LATIN AMERICAN STUDIES

VOLUME 20

Johannes Wilbert, *Editor*

The Evolution of Law in the Barrios of Caracas

by
Kenneth L. Karst
Murray L. Schwartz
Audrey J. Schwartz

Latin American Center
UNIVERSITY OF CALIFORNIA • LOS ANGELES
1973

Acknowledgments

This study was jointly sponsored by the UCLA Latin American Center and by the Centro Latinoamericano de Venezuela (CLAVE). To Johannes Wilbert, who directs UCLA's Center and who was one of the founders of CLAVE, our debt is enormous. Juan M. Guevara B. directed CLAVE during the time when the study was being organized and when the field work was done. We are grateful for his unfailing support and for his personal attention to us and to our work in Caracas. Both in conception and in operation, CLAVE is an extraordinary institution. To CLAVE's then directors—Juan Guevara, George Hall, and Johannes Wilbert—we express our gratitude and our affection.

Two young Venezuelan sociologists, Guillermo Boza and Luis Llambí, were of inestimable importance to the study. They assisted in the construction of the pilot survey questionnaire, conducted the pilot survey, worked with us in putting the questionnaire in final form, obtained crucial documentary data from a great many public and private sources, and led the two teams of interviewers. It is not enough merely to express our thanks to them, but they will understand.

Our participant-observers, who lived in three barrios during the summer of 1967 and whose vivid reports both confirm and complement the statistical evidence of the survey, were: Leon Kaplan, Walter Szczepanek, and Terrence Timmins. The photographs were taken by Kelly Szczepanek.

Jane Trapnell assisted in the preparation of the initial questionnaire, translated our final questionnaire into the English version that appears in this book's Appendix and helped in the preparation of the code. Hilda Morse assisted in preparing the code and directed the process of coding.

We were fortunate in having various drafts of the questionnaire criticized by Kalman Silvert of New York University and by Gabriela Bronfenmajer and Anders Hallstrom of the Centro de Estudios del Desarrollo (CENDES) of the Central University of Venezuela. Our understanding of the dynamics of the city of Caracas was aided very significantly by our conversations with Anthony Penfold of the Oficina Ministerial del Transporte.

We are grateful for the financial support of the "Venezuela 2000" project conducted by the Centro del Estudio del Futuro de Venezuela of the Andrés Bello Catholic University in Caracas.

Our interviewers, then sociology students at the Andrés Bello Catholic University, were: Marixa Andreani, Amalia Barrios, Ernesto Borges, Guillermo Boza (team leader), Vanessa Cartaya, Beatriz Cobo, Beatriz Febres, Augusto Galli, María Pilar García (team leader), Tamara García, Pedro Luis Ghinaglia (team leader), Dyna Guitán, Ernesto Herrera, Luis Llambí (team leader), Humberto Oropeza, María Engracia Paez, Miguel Angel Perera, Lila Siegert, Aurelia Smirneudis, Ligia Soto, Andrés Stambouli, Morelia Tovar, and Blanca Viso.

We wish also to express our appreciation to Ian Kennedy for his perceptive criticisms of a draft of this manuscript. While we may not agree with all his observations, we are confident that the final product is significantly better than that which he graciously reviewed for us.

Finally, we are grateful for the assistance of the following advisers: Dr. Jeannette Abouhamad, Mr. Michael Agar, Dr. José Luis Aguilar, Dr. Arístides Calvani, Dr. Rolando Groscours, Dr. Luis Lander, and Dr. Gustavo Planchart. All of them were most generous in taking time from their heavy responsibilities in order to counsel us and to facilitate the study.

K.L.K.
M.L.S.
A.J.S.

Contents

Introduction

When the world of social science became aware of the urban squatter settlements in Latin America, its early reaction was one of revulsion at the squalor, degradation and poverty in which the teeming multitudes of these rural migrants appeared to live.[1] It was assumed that these areas would continue to decay—if that were possible—and that the residents would have to move out of the settlements if they were to improve their standard of living and become integrated into the larger society.[2]

More recent studies of these settlements have reached different and more optimistic conclusions, pointing out that these settlements typically improve in their physical characteristics and that their residents typically become more integrated into the life of the city with the passage of time.[3]

This book is concerned with one aspect of life in twelve barrios[4] (urban squatter settlements) of Caracas, Venezuela: the expectations which the residents have with respect to property ownership, family relations, commercial dealings, protection against physical invasion, and community organization. In concentrating on these themes, we were concerned with the extent to which they reflected an established legal order within the barrios. They are, after all, notions and concepts that are found in developed legal systems and which anthropologists, under the rubric of "customary law," report upon in their examination of the most primitive cultures.

We embarked upon the study with two interlocking hypotheses. The first was that those persons who lived in the barrios of Caracas

---

[1]See the summary of the early literature in William Mangin, "Latin American Squatter Settlements: A Problem and a Solution," *Latin American Research Review,* (Summer, 1967), 65.

[2]This hypothesis came out of the "Chicago theory" of urban sociology. See generally Robert E. Park and Ernest W. Burgess, *Introduction to the Science of Sociology,* (2nd ed.; Chicago: University of Chicago Press, 1924).

[3]See Mangin, *supra* note 1.

[4]The word *barrio* means "neighborhood" in Spanish. In Venezuela the word refers to a marginal squatter settlement. A non-barrio neighborhood in Caracas is called an *urbanización.*

had, in the main, recently migrated from a rural environment and had brought the culture of that environment to the barrios with them. We were interested in examining—from the standpoint of its impact upon the legal order—the result of the confrontation of that culture with the urban environment in the circumstances of barrio life.

Clearly, a full answer to this question requires a study, over a period of time, of at least the rural environment, the city external to the barrios, and the barrios. The available resources made that comprehensive effort impossible. The study was perforce limited to an examination of the barrios of Caracas. However, to gain some insight into the specific problem of the interaction between the assumedly rural culture and the external environment over a period of time, we selected barrios of markedly different ages as the subjects of the study.

As it turned out, this first hypothesis of the rural backgrounds of those who lived in the barrios proved less well-founded than anticipated. About half of those interviewed[5] (either the heads of households or their spouses) had grown up in towns of over 20,000 population, with almost two-thirds of that group having grown up in Caracas itself. Indeed, only 8 percent of the interviewees grew up in a "village or countryside"; 47 percent grew up in a "pueblo" with a population somewhere between a village and a town of over 20,000.

Our second hypothesis was that the system of order by which the barrios were regulated was distinct from that of the external world and furthermore that it was a product principally of the background of the rural residents, with their own indigenous code of customary law.

The evidence cited above about the origins of those who lived in the barrios makes it difficult, however, to argue confidently that there is a separate system of transplanted indigenous customary law that dominates the law of the barrios. This is not to say, if indeed there are special legal concepts associated with a traditional rural culture, that these concepts may not have had some influence in determining the expectations of the barrio residents. It is to say, however, that in the barrios of Caracas we studied, that separate impact was not discerned.

[5]See pp. 85-88 for a description of the methodology of the study.

What then determines the expectations within the barrios—their emergence and regulation? Is it an autonomous system of order based in part on the rural past, in part on the system of the external community, and in part on the special needs of the barrios? Though this model may have some validity, it cannot easily be demonstrated, for, as will be seen, the resulting system is substantially similar to the national legal system itself.

Whatever their origin, and whether, as discussed below, these common expectations and the system ordering them can properly be characterized as "law," it is indisputably clear from the study that the barrios are not, as some have suggested, a "jungle." Indeed, they appear to be relatively orderly communities in which the residents are upwardly mobile in the socio-economic sense and politically aware as well. The barrio resident does not live in constant fear of his neighbor, the stranger, or the outside world. Rather, he has well-defined expectations, commonly held throughout the barrio, that are not importantly different from what would unquestionably be found in other areas of the city where the residents are of a higher socio-economic status.

Before we examine these topics in detail, we should make our position clear. We choose to identify what we have found in the barrios as a system of "law." We find that there are strongly and commonly held expectations and obligations within a system properly called a legal system. We are aware that the identification of "law" is a matter of considerable debate. We shall not essay a protracted consideration of this jurisprudential issue here. It would involve an attempt to fit the data within the conceptual framework of one or another of the various schools of jurisprudence.[6] The very existence of a variety of such schools indicates that such an effort would not be conclusive.

We are content to state our basic question as follows: Can a system of "law" be identified in the barrios according to some, if not all, of the accepted criteria of a legal system, or is there a system of control by men such that regulation depends not on reason, rules and sanctions, but on the exercise of power in a series of *ad hoc* situations? As stated above, we opt for an analysis that would call what we have found, "law."

[6]A recent, major addition to the debate—and a highly influential one—is Herbert L. A. Hart, *The Concept of Law,* (Oxford: Clarendon Press, 1961). Chapter 5 is particularly relevant to the questions addressed here.

3

During the early years of the barrio's growth at least, there is a body, the junta, which renders decisions in a number of limited but important areas that in other contexts would be considered "legal." Although the junta may not have the full force of, or be comparable to, the external law in carrying out its mandates, it does have the acceptance of the community during this period and is able to implement its decisions. Any lack of formal sanctioning power the junta may have is compensated for by resort to the external legal sanctioning institutions, e.g., the police, which thereby become a part of the fabric of the barrio's institutions. Furthermore, in most cases, in less than a decade the barrio begins to merge with the external environment in these respects. Indeed, in many respects the barrio becomes merely another suburb of the city over time—with all that follows from that integration.

A final theme that was explored and is explicated in detail in the pages that follow (Chapter 8) is the interplay between law and development. If we are correct in characterizing what we have found as a legal system, there is, in our view, a most significant interrelationship between law on the one hand and both the stability and development of the barrios on the other.

The study had three sources of data: (1) a "documentary" search of earlier and contemporaneous descriptions and analyses of barrio life, including scholarly books and articles, official reports, and ephemeral unofficial commentary; (2) the reports of three participant-observers, who lived in three different barrios during the summer of 1967; and (3) a survey questionnaire, with all interviews conducted in ten barrios during the same summer. The text that follows is in the main written in the present tense. The "present," for this purpose, is the year of the study: 1967. The Appendices contain a methodological discussion, a copy of the questionnaire, and the distribution of responses.

We begin with a profile of the barrios and then discuss in turn the results of the study in the five subject areas examined. In the aggregate, these chapters provide a picture of the "law" of the barrios, treated according to our previous discussion. We then examine the changes that are produced over the years between a barrio's initial formation and consolidation and its eventual absorption into the city. Finally, we seek to relate the findings in our diverse subject areas to some general propositions concerning the role of the law of the barrios in the process of development.

1. The Barrios of Caracas

The runways at the Caracas airport run east and west because there is no alternative. The airport runs along a strip of flat land edged by high mountains (8000 feet) on the south and by the Caribbean on the north. The deplaning visitor encounters the tropics: warm, moist air and lush vegetation. But to get to the main city, the visitor must leave the coast and drive fifteen miles up through a mountain pass and down into the valley of Caracas. Here, at an altitude of 2500 feet, the stifling air of the coast is gone, replaced by an "eternal spring" that is more than a promotional slogan.

The valley, also on an east-west axis, is about twenty miles long and ranges from one to five miles in width. It is virtually filled by the city of Caracas. Several smaller valleys open out to the south, and they too are rapidly filling. The northern edge of the city plays out against the steep mountain range that separates the city from the coast. By 1966, greater Caracas had reached a population of nearly 1,800,000, almost one-fifth of the national population. In 1950, the comparable figure was just under 800,000. The city's population is growing at a rate of 6.6 percent per year; for Venezuela as a whole, the annual population growth rate is 3.4 percent. The best estimates are that in 1990 Caracas will be a city of 3.5 to 4.0 million inhabitants. The valley, of course, does not get any bigger. Land prices in Caracas are already very high and will go higher as high-rise apartments replace single-family residences. In 1966, some 35 percent of the city's residents lived in multi-family buildings, and 40 percent lived in "regular" (non-barrio) single-family units. In 1990, these percentages are expected to shift markedly, to 65 percent in multi-family units and 10 percent in "regular" single-family units.

Both the 1966 percentages and the 1990 estimates leave 25 percent of the population unaccounted for. These 25 percent (the percentage is ultra-conservative) live, and their 1990 successors are expected to live, in the barrios, most of them squatting on land for which they do not have title and living in houses built without building permits. The land they occupy is, for the most part, marginal in a physical sense—located mainly on hillsides, but

5

also tucked away in such places as the banks of a stream running below street level, or under a viaduct, or even alongside a new freeway. Some barrios are within easy walking distance of centers of employment and commerce, but others lie on the fringes of the city. A smaller barrio may include only 100 houses; a very large one will house more than 2000 families. There are over 400 barrios in Caracas; some have existed for more than thirty years, and new ones are constantly forming.

Formation of the Barrios

High national rates of population growth alone obviously cannot fully explain the dramatic increase in the population of the barrios. The additional explanation lies in a rapid acceleration of rural-to-urban migration, as Latin America shares a worldwide tendency typically related to improved communications between the metropolis and the provinces. Most studies show that the resident heads of families are largely non-urban in origin but that most of them have lived for a while in the city before coming to the barrios where they now live. One frequent pattern looks something like this: The young man in the countryside or a small town comes with his wife and child to the city to live with relatives. He moves with his family to the barrio after a few years of city residence, and further children are born after the move to the barrio. Those migrants who do move directly into the barrio tend to live with relatives or at least to learn of the availability of land or a house from relatives who already live in the barrio. The pattern of migration thus rests in great part on the flow of information about housing opportunities.

To speak of the "availability" of land is to use a neutral term to describe a situation that normally is characterized by conflict and often results in violence. Squatters, by definition, live on land owned by someone else. Most of the Caracas barrios have originated in "invasions"—rapid (even overnight) occupations by groups of settlers who may or may not have been organized for the occasion. While some such invasions are tolerated and even encouraged by government officials, others are resisted by the government to the point of destruction of the settlers' houses. It is not unusual to hear of a squatter settlement that has been constructed overnight, torn down by the police the next day, constructed again the following night, destroyed again, and reconstructed until the authorities tire of fighting.

When title to vacant land is clearly held by a private individual, the governments have tended to be rather firmly committed to protecting the land against invasion by squatters. When the land is held by the church or by some branch of the government itself, official tolerance is more likely, as it is when the title to "private" land is disputed among several claimants.

For many of Latin America's great cities, large-scale migration and large marginal squatter settlements are phenomena that date from the time of World War II; some of Rio's *favelas* are much older. In Caracas there were barrios in substantial numbers by 1930. But the critical dates in the formation of the Caracas barrios are 1958-60. The military dictatorship of Marcos Pérez Jiménez had sought, during the 1950s, to end the existence of the barrios that had already formed in Caracas and to prevent the formation of new barrios. From 1954 to 1958, the government built apartment houses, including eighty-five *superbloques* (giant fifteen-story apartment buildings), to house 180,000 people. The government's solution to the barrios was the bulldozer. On a given morning, policemen and trucks would arrive at the barrio; an official would direct the loading of the residents' belongings onto the truck; policemen would deal with any objections; when the belongings and the residents had been removed to the new apartments, the houses were demolished. Nevertheless, in 1958, after these upheavals, the barrio population in Caracas was still 220,000.

After the overthrow of Pérez Jiménez in 1958, a provisional junta governed for a year; elections were held in December, 1958, and President Rómulo Betancourt took office two months later. During its brief period of government, the junta put into operation an Emergency Plan, providing for payment of a minimum "wage" to unemployed workers in Caracas. The plan also provided materials and other assistance for public-works projects in the barrios in what seemed at the time to be a makeshift political response to the revolutionary potential of the urban poor. About the same time the plan was activated, the police and the military stopped preventing the formation of new barrios. Thus the principal barrier blocking migration to Caracas was removed, and the system of unemployment compensation for workers in Caracas

7

was a special attraction to migrants. The building materials provided by the government were often pilfered and converted, by this private initiative, into an investment in barrio housing rather than public works. The total city population grew by 400,000 in a single year. By 1966, the residents of the barrios totalled nearly half a million.

Physical Characteristics of the Barrios

It is possible to find some barrios in Caracas that lie on flat land, but the overwhelming majority of the barrios occupy hillsides. The small valleys that open from Caracas to the south are, of course, separated by hills and ridges, most of which are covered with barrios. The hilly eastern and western ends of the main valley are dominated by barrios. Some older barrios occupy low hills right in the middle of the city. The slopes vary in steepness of grade, but nearly all barrio residents live on hills. Perhaps they lack the spectacular panoramas of the Rio *favela* that served as a setting for the movie *Black Orpheus,* but the views of the Valley of Caracas from many barrios are beautiful in the eye of any beholder.

A picture of a "typical" Caracas barrio would show the barrio filling a dish-shaped area on a hillside between two small ridges that run from the top of the hill to the bottom. On the opposite side of each ridge, there is another barrio with a different name. At the bottom of the hill runs a paved street. At a right angle to the street, a short paved street runs up the hill into the barrio for some fifty yards. Beyond the end of this short street, no automobile can pass. There are, however, a few paved stairways that go about two-thirds of the way up the hillside. Halfway up one of these stairways, the pedestrian crosses a level paved walkway that goes in a semicircular path from one side of the barrio to the other. At the top of the stairway there is another such paved path. The resulting pedestrian grid resembles the pattern of the aisles of an open-air amphitheater. Within the grid, the houses are very close together; at the bottom, near the main street, many of the houses have common walls, and some of them are two-story buildings. Concrete walls and concrete ceilings characterize the houses in the lower, more dense sector. Toward the top of the hill, the houses are of poorer

8

construction, and many of them are shacks (*ranchos*) with packing-box sides and zinc roofs. The housing density decreases as the elevation gets higher.

Almost all the houses have electricity; the exceptions are the shacks at the top of the hill. The national government has provided not only the heavy equipment and building materials for constructing the paved walkways and stairways but also pipes for bringing water to the barrio. The houses nearest the street are individually connected to the public water system; the upper reaches of the barrio are served by faucets used commonly by anyone who needs water. For the past month, a construction project has been underway in the barrio; the junta has secured the government's cooperation in building a sewage system. Work proceeds every day, but is especially active on the days when the heavy equipment is available and on weekends. Sewers were installed in the lower portions of the barrio several years ago, and the current project will serve the middle levels. Residents of the upper level will be without sewers for at least two years. The only telephones are in stores that front on the street that runs along the lower edge of the barrio.

An elementary school was built for the barrio five years ago; it is now overflowing, and the school authorities are considering closing the first grade in order to add a sixth grade. Older children must take the bus to their secondary school; the bus stops in front of the barrio. There is no police station in the barrio; the nearest station is a fifteen-minute drive away. There is no dispensary in the barrio, nor is there a pharmacy. The nearest church is two miles away.

The barrio, with a population of 2000, has 350 houses. Its total area is less than ten acres. In the barrio, there are many little stores that sell basic food items, soft drinks and beer, and commodities like soap and small housewares. On the main street at the bottom of the hill there is a bakery, an auto mechanic's shop, a barber shop, and a grocery store that is larger than the little stores on the hillside.

A Socio-Economic Profile of the Barrios

The average barrio house has six occupants. In a barrio near one of the city's centers, the typical house completely fills a lot measuring seven yards wide and ten yards long and perhaps shares a common wall with the adjacent house. In a barrio on the fringes of the city, the house has the same dimensions but is located on a lot that has room for growing flowers or vegetables. Dogs, cats and chickens abound, but other animals are rare.

In the 1967 survey, 46 percent of the interviewees had grown up (spent the ages five to fifteen) in cities of over 20,000 population; almost two-thirds of these (28%) had grown up in Caracas itself.[1] Seven out of eight interviewees had lived in the Caracas barrios for four years or more, and one out of four had lived in the barrios for twenty-two years or more. The median period during which the interviewee had lived in his or her present barrio was four to six years; in the four oldest barrios, the median for this figure was in the range of twelve to thirteen years. Fifty-four percent of the respondents had lived in their present houses for four years or more; 32 percent had lived there for seven years or more; and 22 percent had lived in the same house for ten years or more. In the four oldest barrios, the latter figure (occupancy of the same house for at least ten years) was 47 percent. Despite this high degree of residential permanence, when the interviewees were asked whether they intended to move during the coming year, 35 percent answered affirmatively and only 48 percent negatively. The affirmative answers principally reflected dissatisfaction with physical aspects of the interviewees' present situation (e.g., the desire for a better house, the physical condition of the barrio, the wish of renters to own their own houses) and only secondarily related to "moral" qualities of the barrio environment (e.g., "it is bad for the children here").

In all but the largest barrios, nearly everyone is acquainted with everyone else; even in a barrio of 10,000 residents, there is more familiarity with the neighbors than would be expected in an upper-middle-class *urbanización.*

The strong ties between mother and children warrant classification of the family as matrifocal; yet, four out of five families are headed by men, and in 78 percent of the households, husbands

---

[1]The others had grown up in the Central States (26%), the Andes (20%), the East (11%), the West (9%), the Plains (4%), the Guayana region (1%), or other countries (2%). There was no noticeable tendency for natives of a particular region to concentrate in particular barrios. Thus there are no "regional associations" in the barrios. See Appendix B for the questionnaire and distribution of responses.

live with their wives. The median number of children living in the house is four. Although the basic pattern of occupancy is that of the nuclear family, in a substantial number of households there are deviations from this pattern, primarily those of the absence of the male head of the household or the addition of other relatives: parents, brothers and sisters, nieces and nephews.

One-quarter of the heads of families are illiterate, but the median has completed between four and six years of school. One out of ten heads of families has gone to secondary school or an equivalent, such as a special commercial school. The children have more schooling. Only 3 percent of the children of school age or beyond are illiterate; at least one out of three has attended secondary school or its equivalent. These educational statistics are reflected in the everyday conversation of the barrio residents. While they tend to have only modest expectations for themselves in the way of socio-economic advancement, they are very optimistic about their children. Education is seen as the road to progress for the individual and for the community.

After just a few years of existence, a barrio sprouts television antennas. Barrio residents generally read the newspapers, and virtually every family has a small radio. Two music-and-news radio stations in Caracas specialize in public-service announcements about the barrios, such as "Radio Rumbo calls on the responsible authorities to act on the petition of the Barrio Brisas de Pro Patria for immediate establishment of a dispensary." The very existence of such an announcement suggests a certain sophistication on the part of the barrio residents—mastery of some of the public-relations techniques of the modern urban political system.

In only one household in ten is no one employed. Where the head of the family is unemployed (as in 28 percent of the households—more frequently where the head of the family is a woman), children or other relatives support the household. Employment ranges over a variety of occupations but centers on five categories: (a) skilled labor (e.g., auto mechanic, building-trades specialist); (b) unskilled labor (including drivers of Caracas's fixed-line jitney cabs); (c) low-level white-collar employment; (d) domestic employment; and (e) government employment (e.g., policeman, messenger for a federal agency).[2]

---

[2]The unemployment rate for Caracas as a whole was 13 percent at the time of the study. As is generally true of these types of employment, there was probably a high rate of underemployment.

Measuring family living standards by monthly expenditures—admittedly an imprecise index—the median expenditure per household is 500-799 Bolívars per month. Since the Bolívar is worth about $.22 (U.S.), the median monthly family expenses range from $110 to $175. Caracas is notoriously an expensive city in which to live, but even so, this level of expenditure by no means represents miserable poverty.

The Diversity of the Barrios

The foregoing profiles emphasize composite descriptions and average percentages. It should not, however, be forgotten that the barrios are diverse in their ages, populations, physical characteristics, level of community organization, and other socio-economic characteristics.[3] The following descriptions of the individual barrios demonstrate this diversity.

La Amapola, the oldest barrio studied, is situated in the parish of Caracas called La Vega in one of the valleys leading out of the Valley of Caracas to the south. Old maps show La Vega as a separate town, but the parish has long been regarded as part of the city of Caracas. The oldest barrios in Caracas are to be found in La Vega. La Amapola was founded in about 1925 and had filled its steep hillside by 1933. It is surrounded by other barrios, but its boundary lines are indistinct. At the end of a short paved road into the barrio, stairways ascend the hill. La Amapola is a poor barrio with some 210-220 houses of varying quality. The barrio junta is inactive. However, the juntas in two adjoining barrios joined in organizing the residents of La Amapola for the purpose of obtaining various public services. A water project, under the direction of the juntas of the two adjoining barrios and with the assistance of technicians from the National Institute of Sanitary Works, was underway on the day the interviewers surveyed the residents of La Amapola. Residents of La Amapola were providing labor and contributing money for the project.

San Miguel is located within a mile of Petare, the population center of the eastern end of the Valley of Caracas. This barrio was

---

3For a careful analysis of the dimensions of the kind of diversity here suggested, see Anthony Leeds, "The Significant Variables Determining the Character of Squatter Settlements," *América Latina,* 12 (July-Sept., 1969), 44.

first settled as long ago as 1932 but dates mainly from 1945. It is integrated into the city of Caracas in a physical sense, with the great majority of its 200 houses within a block of a paved street (paved since 1945) that runs up and over the hill on which the barrio is situated. (This street joins Avenida Miranda, the principal artery of the east end of the city.) Almost all the houses are of concrete-block construction, and many are coated with stucco and paint; the area is losing its "barrio look." The population has been stable since 1959. There is excellent communication (at the top of the hill) with the barrio on the other side of the hill, where there are a church, a school and a dispensary. The land on one side of the main street was formerly owned by three private owners; after occupying the lands, many residents bought their parcels from these owners. The land on the other side of the street is owned by the government agency responsible for much low-cost housing in Caracas; the agency is selling parcels of land on the installment plan. Family incomes are relatively high in San Miguel. There is a barrio junta, headed by an organizer for Acción Democrática, one of the major national political parties. The junta president is frequently away from the barrio on party business, but the junta nonetheless is active, having recently organized at the time of the survey a project to bring water to houses that are off the main street. There are active juvenile gangs, and the residents consider the barrio to have a "tough" reputation.

Marín, a larger-than-average barrio (450 houses) located in the heart of Caracas, dates from 1927, although much of the barrio's area became covered with houses only after World War II. The barrio, despite its location, has surprisingly poor communication with the city's employment and commercial centers. It is cut off from the civic center by the Guaire River and a freeway. The barrio in its physical characteristics resembles the composite barrio described earlier in this chapter. The houses along the main street at the bottom of the hill are not regarded as part of the barrio. The steep hills of the higher zones are covered by ranchos, and this area is considered to be "tough." There is no longer any barrio junta.

Quebrada Catuche, as its name suggests, is stretched along the stream bed of the Catuche River for about a mile. The Catuche is now all but dry, its remaining water stagnant and unpleasant to the nose. The barrio stands in the northwest part of the valley

13

below ground level. Standing in the barrio, one looks up some fifty to seventy-five feet to see the bridges that cross the river bed, connecting streets in the oldest part of Caracas. It is cool and shady—and depressing. There is a sense of isolation from the city, although major streets are directly overhead. Many of the 160 houses are of very poor quality, although some are quite substantial, even several stories high. The barrio was founded in the late 1930s but did not assume its present size until after World War II. There is no barrio junta and virtually no sense of community, although two of the national political parties maintain modest headquarters in two of the houses.

El Desvío, a relatively prosperous barrio of around 210 houses, is an offshoot of a larger barrio called La Bandera, founded around 1940. The barrio is located on a steep hill that is served by a paved road that gives way after two blocks to a system of cement stairways and terraces. Many of the buildings are of several stories; the barrio is densely populated, and houses are in good condition. Family incomes here are the highest in all the barrios studied. There is excellent access to the city; a major thoroughfare runs along the bottom of the hill. The junta is active and well regarded by the residents.

Niño Jesús is located at the far western end of the valley, off the highway to Junquito. While there are some 340 houses, the houses are set apart from one another, and the barrio has a distinctly rural atmosphere. From the barrio, the view encompasses the hills surrounding the main highway from Caracas down to the sea. The barrio, atypically, goes *down* the hill from the highway. The road into the barrio is paved at the entrance, but only for a short distance. In the barrio's lower, newer sectors, some of the roads are not passable by automobiles. Although family incomes here are relatively high, many of the houses are of wood. The barrio was founded in 1950, when the first resident bought his parcel from the owner of a larger tract of land, and others soon followed his example. On one side of the main road into the barrio, virtually all the residents have bought their land in this fashion. On the other side of the road, where title to the land has been in dispute among four or five claimants, the residents have simply occupied the land without buying it. A junta organized by one of the national political parties shortly after the fall of Pérez Jiménez was soon dissolved. A new junta, with which the residents have been cooperative, now exists. It has produced both water and electricity for the barrio; a sewage project is planned; a women's committee runs a kindergarten.

Aguacaticos, founded around 1960, is a medium-sized barrio (200 houses) that runs along a draw, uphill from another older barrio. Aguacaticos is southeast of Petare, along the highway that winds its way out of the Valley of Caracas to the east. Houses completely fill the draw, standing on both sides of a steep street that runs up the hill. At the end of the paved street, there are a number of houses that are reachable only on foot. Although most of the houses (except for the ones at the uppermost end of the barrio) are constructed of concrete blocks, few of the houses have the look of city houses. There is much more of the distinctive "barrio look" here than in, for example, San Miguel, which is not far away. A new junta had recently taken office when the interviewers went to Aguacaticos. Road repairs, under the new junta's sponsorship, were underway.

La Silsa is an enormous barrio (2000 houses) that sprawls over a hill just south of Catia Square at the western end of Caracas. The barrio was founded in 1960 and named for the big Silsa dairy that stands at the base of the hill. (SILSA stands for Sindicato Lecherero, S.A.) The houses toward the bottom of the hill are mostly of concrete block, and many are covered with stucco and paint. There are many roads through the barrio and considerable vehicular traffic, although the roads are paved only near the two main entrances at the bottom of the hill. The barrio is only a few blocks from a major commercial center; there is no sense of isolation from the city here. Because the barrio is so large, there are seven identifiable subsectors, including one *"zona roja"* that is regarded as politically leftist. Nonetheless, a single junta governs barrio affairs throughout all the zones. In classifying the barrios according to their respective ages, La Silsa was divided; the upper portion was classified among the newest barrios. There is some sectional rivalry and some talk among the residents of the uphill zones of the formation of a separate junta. The current junta is moderately active; it has strong connections with one of the national political parties. One of the participant-observers lived in La Silsa and assisted the junta in preparing a barrio census.

Guzmán Blanco was founded in 1964, only three years before the survey was conducted. The barrio is set in a dish-shaped valley, uphill from a highway that runs out of the Valley of Caracas to the southwest. It is popularly known as La Chivera, named after an automobile parts business at the base of the hill; one first sees the barrio over a sea of rusting automobile bodies. The houses are almost all very poor in quality; family incomes run low. Communication with the city is fairly good; buses and fixed-line jitney taxis stop immediately in front of the barrio. The junta is moderately active but has not yet secured much in the way of public services.

Cuatricentenario, only five months old at the time of the survey, was named for the 400th anniversary of the founding of Caracas, celebrated during 1967. It is the most remote from the city of all the barrios studied. Its 140 houses run along a winding paved road, the extension of the highway that runs near Aguacaticos, well east of Petare, and is a long bus ride from any city employment. Most of the residents are from the interior of Venezuela, although some have come from other barrios near Petare. At the time of the survey, the police had not yet stopped harassing the residents, who had been fighting to consolidate the barrio's very existence. The junta had been occupied in this consolidation effort and had not yet brought electricity, water, sewers, or any other public services to the barrio. It was evident that the installation of such services would be very difficult, owing to the scattered pattern of housing development. Cuatricentenario was still very rural in mid-1967. The houses were all ranchos; there had been no time for their improvement. Family incomes here are the lowest in all the barrios studied.

The foregoing descriptions include the ten barrios surveyed by questionnaire. While one of the participant-observers lived in La Silsa, the other two lived in barrios that were not part of the questionnaire survey. Those barrios, *La Charneca* and *Hornos de Cal,* were located alongside Marín, described above, and shared many of that barrio's characteristics. The participant-observer who resided in La Charneca lived in the upper portion of the barrio, where a new junta was formed during his stay and a new barrio name adopted for the newly separated hilltop barrio. This phenomenon is discussed in Chapter 6.

2. Rights in Land and Housing

General Juan Vicente Gómez, the archetypal early-twentieth-century Latin American military dictator, died in 1935. His vast landholdings were not divided among his many scores of children but instead were "inherited" by the government. As a result, the title to much of the hillside land in Caracas is formally held by one or another branch of government. The conflicting claims of various levels of government frequently make it impossible to say who, or which public corporate entity, owns the land on which a barrio has formed. Similarly, a considerable proportion of the private land in these marginal areas has been claimed by more than one would-be owner. Despite these uncertainties, some barrio residents have bought the land on which they live, either from the municipality[1] or from private owners. In the 1967 survey, twenty-one percent of the respondents answered that their land was owned by them, by their spouses, or by other relatives; these responses were concentrated in the three oldest barrios of the ten surveyed, where the municipal governments and some private owners have engaged in modest efforts to sell land to the persons occupying it. A similar percentage (19 %) identified other private individuals as the owners of land, but nearly half the respondents said that they did not know who owned the land.[2] These figures are, of course, the statistical reflection of the expression "squatter community." By definition, a squatter lives on someone else's land; the barrio residents who now own their land are more accurately called ex-squatters.

Most lawyers, certainly most Venezuelan lawyers, would conclude that the barrio squatter's position is precarious and insecure. One rather general hypothesis of the barrio study, confirmed by the study's results, was that such a conclusion was not justified. More than four out of five of the interviewees said that they, their spouses, or other relatives owned the houses they were occupying.

[1]Municipal government is complicated in Caracas by the fact that part of the city is in the Federal District and part lies in the Sucre District of the State of Miranda; thus there are two separate city governments.

[2]One elderly lady said to an interviewer that the land in her barrio originally had belonged to Jesus and that he had never sold it to anyone.

17

The rest rented their houses. In the newer barrios, nearly all the occupant families owned their houses. In the older barrios, the percentage of renters increased to as high as 40 percent in one central-city barrio. The older barrios are blending into the city, gradually losing their distinctive "barrio" characteristics, and land titles are becoming regularized.[3] In such a barrio, if an occupant does not own the land on which he is living, he is not likely to own the house either; instead, he is renting from another person who owns both house and land. In the newer barrios, ownership of the house and the land tend to be divided.

Acquisition of Land and Houses

Six out of seven respondents in the 1967 survey came with their families to the barrios in which they were living, and only one-seventh came alone. The motivating force for the move usually is the opportunity to own a home. One barrio resident spoke of his decision to move to the barrio during the early days of the barrio's formation: "I used to come by here every day. Everyone's ambition is to live under his own roof, not in an apartment that belongs to someone else. You have to ask permission for everything—to bring up a bed, to change a plug. Besides, I want to have something to leave to the children, a little house or something like that." The decision to move to a particular barrio is importantly influenced by the presence in the barrio of relatives. That consideration far outranks others, such as convenience to employment or schools or shopping.[4]

While most barrios have been formed by land invasions, only one-sixth of the respondents reported that they had acquired their land by occupation. In the newer barrios, the percentages were

[3]The percentages of "Don't know" answers to the question of land ownership were very low in the older barrios.

[4]Similar motivations are reported for the *barriadas* of Lima, for the *favelas* of Rio, and for a barrio in Ciudad Guayana, Venezuela. Matos Mar, "The 'Barriadas' of Lima: An Example of Integration into Urban Life," in Philip M. Hauser, ed., *Urbanization in Latin America,* (Paris: UNESCO, 1961), 170, 175; Andrew Pearse, "Some Characteristics of Urbanization in the City of Rio de Janeiro," in Hauser, *supra,* 191, 196-199; Lisa R. Peattie, *The View from the Barrio,* (Ann Arbor: University of Michigan Press, 1968), 40. When a couple marry, they expect to move to a separate household. See Peattie, *supra,* at 43.

18

markedly higher, reaching 57 percent in the very newest, which was only five months old at the time of the survey. The point is not that the older barrios were formed more peacefully but rather that the present occupants of older barrios have acquired their occupancy rights by orderly purchase or rental from earlier occupants. It is not unusual for an occupant to report that he has bought his land from another, even when he does not claim legal title. What he means is this: Someone else had been assigned an area of land early in the barrio's history and had carved a level lot out of the hillside, then sold his rights to occupy the lot to the present occupant, who has built a house.

After the invasion has established the initial settlers on the land, the assignment of parcels is the function of the barrio junta, which will have been "elected" from among the first residents to occupy land in the barrio.[5] The junta may or may not be authorized by the municipal government to make the assignment of parcels, but with or without such authority the junta is likely to find that it must take responsibility for lot assignments if it is to exercise any authority in the barrio. Lots are measured—perhaps seven by ten meters in a barrio that is close to the city's commercial and employment centers and fifteen by twenty meters in a more rural setting. A new arrival asks the junta's permission to occupy a lot, perhaps showing a letter from a municipal office authorizing him to move into the barrio.[6] As the barrio becomes established, a weakening junta may abandon this power to designate the parcels of land where new arrivals may build, but a

[5]Talton Ray says that invasion leaders do not control the assignment of lots among invaders of hillside barrios. Talton Ray, *The Politics of the Barrios of Venezuela,* (Berkeley: University of California Press, 1969), 39. Our study did not include any barrio that was in the process of initial formation through invasion. In the newest barrio, however, a majority of the interviewees responded that the junta had supervised the assignment of parcels; this barrio was a hillside barrio. Our findings are reconcilable with the Ray statement if the latter is confined to the invasion stage; by the time a junta has been chosen, the invaders will have been settled, and the junta's supervision of parcel assignments will be limited to new arrivals. In the text, the word "elected" is set off in quotation marks to convey some skepticism about the degree of democracy that goes into the junta's selection. See Ray, *supra,* at 44-45, for a similar view.

[6]Sometimes the letter will come not from a government agency but from a member of the junta in another barrio. Such a request is of little value, except as a demonstration of respect or dignity. But such a demonstration may be important to the man in search of land and to his relatives who live in the barrio that cannot take him. This theme—the dignity that attaches to every human being—is one that runs throughout all the subject areas of our study.

19

strong junta will retain the power as a device to screen out persons thought to be undesirable.

Once the land is acquired, the construction of a house almost always is accomplished by the occupying family itself, frequently with the aid of relatives or neighbors. In the barrios there are some residents who are specially talented in construction and who hire themselves out to assist in some of the more complicated tasks. But at the outset of a barrio's existence, the construction of an invader's shack is not too difficult for him to manage by himself. He needs assistance only later, when he makes improvements that begin to transform a rancho into a structure that is called simply a "house."

Among those who owned their own houses (including ranchos), two-thirds had built their houses, as distinguished from buying them. This figure initially seems inconsistent with the assertion, made previously, that only one-sixth of the respondents to the survey had acquired their land by occupation. The explanation lies in the consistent pattern of investment that characterizes all barrios. The interviewees, for the most part, had built the houses in which they were then living; such a response is consistent with an earlier purchase of a house on the same site, which house has since been entirely replaced.[7]

Once established in a barrio, a family tends to stay there. The median family had been in the same barrio for four to six years, and some 31 percent of the respondents had been where they were then living for ten years or more.

Ownership Rights and the Role of the Junta

The one barrio resident in five who owns his land has the usual rights of ownership; his title will be registered in the appropriate land registry and protected by the full power of Venezuela's formal legal system. In this discussion we are not concerned with such an ex-squatter, but rather with his neighbor who claims ownership of a house, but not of the land under It. Some 60 percent of the barrio residents fit this description. What does it mean to "own" one's house when one is a squatter?

---

[7]Or, alternatively, with the purchase of a lot that has been leveled by its initial occupant, as noted earlier in the text, p. 19.

The most obvious characteristic of ownership is the right to undisturbed possession. In the barrios, a challenge to an owner-occupant's right to remain in his house is a rarity. All but 11 percent of the respondents in the 1967 survey said that no one had ever disputed their rights to build on the land or live in their houses. The percentage of affirmative responses to this question was relatively high (24%) only in the barrio that was five months old at the time of the survey, most of whose residents had taken their land by occupation. Disputes about the right to occupy a parcel occur, if they occur at all, primarily during the early days of the barrio's existence. After a short time, virtually all such disputes cease, and possession is peaceful. Occasionally someone will turn up who claims to represent the true owner of the land (the 11 percent figure above represents these incidents), but the nearly universal reaction to such an appearance has been to reject any demand for removal from the premises or for payment for the land.

Thus, the central fact about a squatter-owner's rights is that nothing happens to disturb his occupancy. The neighbors respect each other's rights; the sense of "yours" and "mine" is accepted and enforced. The enforcement typically happens in one of the rare disputes over boundaries between adjoining neighbors. In such a case, the junta's decision settles the issue. Boundary disputes, like other disputes about the rights of squatter-owners, tend to arise early in the barrio's history and then to cease.

In the oldest barrios, where most houses share common walls with the houses next door, boundary disputes are nearly a physical impossibility. But analogous issues about an owner's rights do arise. For example, suppose that one resident begins to excavate into the hill behind his house for the purpose of adding a room; his neighbor to the rear may be afraid that the digging will undermine his house and may call on the barrio junta to insist on a retaining wall, or to stop the digging altogether. Such a dispute, like a boundary dispute, falls clearly within the junta's customary jurisdiction.

Other claims to rights in land are not infrequently brought before the junta. Sometimes it is hard for a resident to reach his house without passing over the lot of another resident; the typical case would be that of the uphill man who needs to pass over the downhill neighbor's lot. Usually, no trouble would arise. If the

21

two neighbors have a falling out, however, the downhill man may threaten violence to the uphill man who tries to cross his lot. In such a case, the junta may order that a right-of-way be given. (This problem is apt to be as temporary as the usual boundary dispute. Even if the neighbors perpetuate their feud, the matter may be resolved by the building of a common concrete stairway.)

The boundary dispute and the "easement" case are the clearest examples of conflicts that come within the customary judicial power of the junta. There is, in fact, a relation between the junta's judicial power and its legislative power over rights in land. The settlement of a conflict over boundaries is a logical outgrowth of the power to allocate vacant parcels. Once a house is built on a lot, however, the junta will not seek to control the owner in his sale of the house to another.[8] However, in extreme cases of nuisance, where an occupant is seriously interfering with his neighbors' use of land, the junta may try to expel the offender from the barrio. Even a strong junta may not be able to make such a sanction stick if the resident who is the subject of the expulsion effort is well connected in the municipal government. Absent such influence, however, a strong junta will have the power to expel, provided that the offender does not have title to his land. The expelled owner of a house would be permitted to sell it as he pleased; the junta would not veto occupancy by the buyer.

Expulsion, obviously, is an extremely severe sanction to be applied only in extreme circumstances. A noisy radio, for example, may simply be tolerated without even a complaint by the neighbors.[9] Domestic quarrels that produced excessive noise might result in an effort by the junta to quiet the combatants, but would have to cause some fear of violence to justify expulsion.[10] Open defiance of the barrio's customary standards of morality, such as the operation of a house of prostitution, has resulted in expulsion. Continued violation of the junta's rules about trash disposal is also a serious offense; the junta knows that garbage may

---

[8]The rental of a rancho (a substandard house) is another matter. See text at note 12, *infra*.

[9]Such an incident, reported by Peattie, *supra* note 4, at 59, had an exact parallel in one of the barrios included in our study. The issue appears to be one of respect; see note 6, *supra*.

[10]Generally, a domestic quarrel is beyond the junta's "jurisdiction," unless it interferes unduly with the neighbors' enjoyment of their land.

22

breed not only flies but also violence. These standards—these informal rules of law—are examples of the barrios' most distinctive contribution to the law that effectively governs the barrios, and they are worked out case by case.

The barrio house-owner's right to transfer his house is universally recognized by his neighbors. He can sell the house or give it away, and the transferee's right to occupy will not be challenged. (If the house should remain vacant for a period of several months, the junta may assign another family to occupy it. An even longer period of vacancy would be respected, however, if it were understood that the transferee had been delayed in taking possession by, say, illness.) Alternatively, the owner may rent his house; about one house in five in the barrios is rented.

If an owner's occupancy of his house were precarious, the owner's death would likely produce some instability. In fact, the nearly universal result upon the death of the owner of a barrio house is the assumption of ownership rights by members of his family. The responses to the 1967 survey showed that almost everyone expected to be able to designate the successor to his interest in his house, and over 98 percent said they expected to leave their belongings, including their houses, to relatives. While nine out of ten barrio residents had taken no action to assure their families of the right of succession, about half of them expressed the intention to do so, usually in vague terms about "signing a document" of some sort. A few who said they had no intention of taking any action to assure the passage of their property to their children remarked that there was no need to do so since the children were legitimate.[11] That view, which may have been held by others who did not volunteer a reason for their lack of intention to make a will or otherwise control the succession to their property, reflects an awareness of the national legislation about inheritance.

---

[11]On termination of an informal union, the house generally goes to the spouse who built it (or had it built, or bought it). It is not unknown, however, for the wife to lose a house that was hers before the commencement of the union; the junta is apt to characterize such a dispute as a domestic dispute and thus beyond its proper power.

Rental Arrangements

The rental of a rancho—a substandard shack—is specifically prohibited by national law.[12] The result of the law is that the tenant of a rancho need not pay rent, and if such payments are made, theoretically he has a right to recover them. This right, however, depends on the characterization of the house as a rancho; a tenant may apply to a national government agency for a certificate reflecting a determination that the house is substandard and authorizing the tenant to remain in possession without paying rent. The owner, on the other hand, may apply to the same agency for a certificate that his house is adequately constructed, entitling him to collect rent from a tenant.

The regulations, it will be seen, rely on agencies of the government for their enforcement; there is no place in the regulatory scheme for the barrio junta to play any role. In other respects, however, a strong junta will be exercising jurisdiction over matters relating to rights in land, and it is not surprising that some juntas assert the additional power to police illegal rentals of ranchos. The form of the policing is simple; the junta prevents the landlord from evicting the tenant for nonpayment of rent. One member of a junta put it this way: If the owner rents his rancho, then he doesn't need it, and someone who needs it should have it. Presumably this attitude was not what motivated the government to prohibit the rental of ranchos; the regulation seems instead to have been adopted in order to discourage the business of building ranchos in order to rent them. Still, the two purposes often lead to the same result—relieving the tenant from paying rent. So the public authorities have not obstructed the juntas from assisting.

Thus a tenant can move into a rancho, paying the first month's rent; instead of going through the procedure of getting a certificate from the government, he can simply inform the junta, which will protect him from the landlord's harassment. Some juntas have made similar efforts to stop builder-speculators who construct ranchos and then sell them, but the junta's power to reach such cases is more limited. Ranchos can be built, sold and occupied practically overnight, and the junta will not be

12*Reglamento de la Ley de Regulación de Alquileres y del Decreto Legislativo sobre Desalojo de Vivienda* (1960), art. 21-25.

24

disposed to evict the buyer once he and his family are in the rancho.

The proportion of rented houses appears to be correlated positively with the age of the barrio; in the 1967 survey, there were many rented houses in the oldest barrios (up to 40%), while in the two barrios most recently formed, the percentages of renters were zero and 1.7 percent, respectively. Since by far the greater number of ranchos is in the newer barrios, it appears that popular practice is in accord with the national legislation. The rancho is for the most part a temporary dwelling to be lived in by the owner until he can modify the building progressively by adding a cement floor, block wall, and a concrete roof.

The terms of the typical rental arrangement are simple and unwritten. The tenant must pay rent; if he fails to pay, he must vacate. (About one-quarter of the tenants do not follow this pattern; most of them appear to be living in houses owned by relatives.) Other conditions are rare, but a substantial number of renters assume that their landlords could evict them for causing damage to the house or for using the house for an illicit purpose. Only in a handful of cases has an owner sought to raise the rent during a tenant's occupancy; the usual pattern seems to be that the landlord does not make improvements for the tenant and therefore does not ask for an increase in rent.

Tenure Security Without Titles

The 1967 survey asked this question of residents who did not own the land on which their houses were located: "If the owner of the land came and asked you to pay him, what would you do?" The answers demonstrate the strength of the barrio residents' expectations of permanence:

18.0%	We would move
3.0%	The owner would have to pay us the value of the house
48.5%	We would pay for the land (without conditions), or we would pay if everyone else did
5.9%	We would pay for the land if he could prove he was the owner

25

7.9%	We would pay for the land if he would set a fair price (or give us time to pay, etc.)
1.0%	We would do whatever the junta said to do
2.6%	We would reach an agreement (without specifying either sale of the house or purchase of the land)
3.3%	We would go to the authorities (or the police, etc.)
9.8%	Don't know

Thus the great majority expected to be able to work out a compromise arrangement in order to stay where they were. The majority's willingness to pay for their land, given the political unlikelihood of eviction, may seem altruistic. An alternative explanation, however, is that the barrio residents are aware of the system of land titles and want the added security of a formally recognized title.

Another question in the survey asked whether the resident would expect to be paid for his house in the event that the government should decide to take his land to build a road. Some 92 percent of the respondents answered affirmatively, and fewer than 2 percent answered negatively. In fact, national law requires government agencies to compensate for squatters' houses in such circumstances—for example, when a tunnel is dug through a hillside, requiring the removal of a barrio's houses[13]—and this law is observed. The residents' sense of security is strong enough for 34 percent of them to answer that they would expect the government to compensate them for their *land* in the case of such a taking; since only 21 percent have title to their land, there are some who think the government would place a compensable value on a squatter's right to occupy someone else's land.

As stated earlier, the barrio residents have come to the barrio principally for the purpose of owning their own houses. Here, as in other marginal squatter settlements in Latin America, the barrio resident who owns his house need not fear eviction for failure to pay rent. In avoiding this major insecurity, however, the migrant to the barrio subjects himself to the insecurities that attach to his squatter status. A concrete measure of the sense of permanence is the resident's investment in his house. The 1967 survey asked this

---

[13]*Ley de Expropiación por Causa de Utilidad Pública o Social* (1959), tit. V, art. 43, provides for compensation to persons who have made improvements on land they do not own, in cases of taking for public use.

question of owners of houses: "Have you added any important additions to the house? If so, what?" (An "important" addition was defined narrowly: a concrete roof, cement-block walls, a cement floor, or another room.) Eliminating the barrio that had been in existence only five months, we find these responses:

25.8%	No
36.9%	Yes, one such improvement
20.0%	Yes, two such improvements
17.3%	Yes, three or more such improvements

Thus, about three-quarters of the barrio homeowners surveyed had made at least one major investment in their houses, and 37 percent had made at least two such improvements. Furthermore, more than 71 percent said that they were planning to make improvements of this kind in the future. The results are visible to the eye. The houses in the newest barrios are nearly all ranchos of carton-and-zinc construction. The older the barrio, the better are its houses. The oldest barrios blend into the city physically; cement-block walls are covered with stucco and painted in pastel colors. The 1967 survey confirmed these impressions, showing markedly better housing construction in the older barrios than in the newer ones. In barrios that have existed for more than a few years, more than two-thirds of the houses have cement-block walls.

Rented houses, on the other hand, are improved far less frequently; some 74 percent of the renters reported no important improvements. Thus, the key to motivation to investment in barrio housing appears to be the occupant's ownership of the house. Ownership of the land seems not to be significant in this process since the responses to questions about investment are nearly the same among home owners in the various barrios, regardless of the presence in some barrios of substantial numbers of residents who have title to their land.

This steady accretion of housing investment—what a young Venezuelan sociologist called "a work of ants"—demonstrates beyond doubt that the barrio residents feel secure in the occupancy of their houses. There are various ways of looking at the idea of security, but the security that is relevant here is the state of mind of the decision-maker. In the present context, in other words, the security that matters is the barrio resident's expectations about the future. We are accustomed to think of the law's contribution to the security of tenure in formal terms; the title to land, established by reference to authoritative documents, gives the owner access to the state's coercive power to protect him against dispossession. The strong sense of security in the barrios, however, plainly does not rest on title. What, then are its sources?

The barrio resident, to feel secure, must be assured against two kinds of threats: those that may arise from within the barrio and those that may come from outside. Neighbors in the barrio do generally respect one another's ownership rights; there is no need to post a guard to defend one's possession. Furthermore, the rights of a barrio house-owner are enforced by the junta in a number of well-defined situations, in a system of community-wide universality and uniformity that, in our terms, is "law."[14]

The external threat to security may present itself in the form of a demand by an agent of the "landowner" for payment or more dramatically in the form of policemen who insist that the barrio residents leave. The residents know, however, that any such external threat depends on the government. The junta makes its ties to one or more political parties to secure governmental support for the barrio's consolidation.[15] (By the time the junta has declined in importance, this brokerage function—political organizing in exchange for governmental services and other support—is obsolete, for the barrio has become established.)

In Caracas, various branches of government have reinforced the sense of security in the barrios, not only by calling off the police but more importantly by providing materials and other assistance in the construction of public-works facilities. The original "owner" of barrio land may have understood that his claims were shaky when the police failed to stop an invasion; he is certain he

---

[14]See Max Rheinstein, ed., *Max Weber on Law in Economy and Society*, (Cambridge, Mass.: Harvard University Press, 1954), 20; compare Marc Galanter, "The Modernization of Law," in Myron Weiner, ed., *Modernization: The Dynamics of Growth*, (New York: Basic Books, 1966), 153, 154-155.

[15]One member of the municipal council that governs the portion of Caracas that is in the Federal District has long regarded himself as the "voice of the barrios." He regularly visits barrios, holding court as the people's tribune. He is regarded by the residents as effective, and he continues to win re-election. For discussion of the relationships among barrios and Venezuela's political parties, see Ray, *supra* note 5, chapters 6 and 7.

has lost when the government prods the electric company into providing service to the new barrio[16] and provides pipes for a water distribution system and cement for stairways. The greatest single contribution to security of tenure in the Caracas barrios has been the Emergency Plan of 1958, which had nothing whatever to do with land titles.[17] Moreover, since only one barrio resident out of nine has ever been confronted with even a claim of payment for his land, it is no wonder that the residents continue to invest in their homes.[18]

This process of investment is fundamental to the process of development treated more extensively in Chapter 8. The decision of the individual head of a barrio household to improve his house may seem insignificant in the development process when compared to the activities of the government

---

[16]See David J. Myers, *The Political Process of Urban Development: Caracas under Acción Democrática*, (Ann Arbor: University Microfilms, 1969), 47 ff.

[17]See p. 7, *supra*. Venezuela has not adopted any general barrio law.

In addition to the Emergency Plan, there was another major governmental program to aid the barrio residents. The Committee to Remodel the Barrios (CRB) was established in 1962, financed largely by AID money. The CRB identified two types of barrios: (a) those which should be converted into stable neighborhoods through government-supported self-help projects, and (b) those which were on unsuitable terrain and should be eradicated. In most of the latter, the terrains were reshaped and ranchos replaced with small apartment buildings (up to four stories), the units of which were rented to people who had lived in the demolished barrio. Other residents of the old barrio, especially those who had the lowest incomes and could not afford to rent the new apartments, were to be relocated. The relocation program was a failure. The CRB program to support self-help programs was criticized by AID officials for failure to guard against pilferage of building materials delivered to barrio sites, failure to keep good records, etc. The vital fact is that the materials were delivered to the barrios and in one form or another were invested in improvements. The CRB self-help program was not neat, but it worked. Nonetheless, for a variety of political reasons the CRB was liquidated in early 1967, soon after President Leoni succeeded President Betancourt. For an excellent analysis of the political history of the CRB, see Myers, *supra* note 16, at 292-424.

For careful and thoughtful analyses of Peruvian and Brazilian legislation dealing with urban squatters in different ways, see Kenneth Manaster, "The Problem of Urban Squatters in Developing Countries: Peru," *Wisconsin Law Review,* (1968), 23, 42, and Stephen Conn, *The Squatters' Rights of Favelados,* Cuaderno no. 32, (Cuernavaca, Mexico: Centro Intercultural de Documentación, 1969), 2, 35.

[18]The 1967 survey did not interview persons outside the barrios and thus did not reach former residents of barrios that had been eradicated. The 1:9 ratio refers only to present residents of barrios. The number of barrios eradicated after 1958 has not been great, but the number of persons relocated by the CRB, see note 17, *supra,* did reach into the thousands. (The present barrio population in Caracas is around 600,000.)

planner who is responsible for the import quotas or the money supply. But there are 100,000 barrio households in Caracas, and the aggregate of these decisions constitutes a considerable development potential, which is continuously being realized. What is important to emphasize here is that it is the security of tenure that makes this process of investment, and in turn this aspect of development, possible.

3. Family Obligations

The extended family's role in supporting migrants to the city from the Latin American countryside is typified by this comment on the *barriadas* of Lima:

> ... it is always the family which provides the greatest source of security for the inhabitants of these areas. Even when very unsettled and living in very overcrowded conditions, the family is always the mainstay of its members. [1]

The great majority of the barrio residents in Caracas have lived for a time in the city before moving to the barrio and thus are not rural migrants when they come to the barrio. Still, the family normally provides the same kind of support for the new barrio resident, and in fact most barrio residents have relatives living in the same barrio. Of the majority of residents who have built their own houses, many have been assisted in the task by relatives. And those who have given or received lodging in a time of emergency report that their benefactors and beneficiaries have been members of the family.

The primary focus of the study in the area of family obligations was on the nuclear family—specifically, the mutual obligations of spouses and the parents' obligations to their children.

Husband and Wife

The great majority of households (about 78%) included a nuclear family of husband, wife, and children. (In 46 percent of the households, only the nuclear family was present; in the others, other relatives were also present.) Where there is a husband present, he is regarded as the head of the family.[2] Among the couples living together, about half described their status as

---

[1]Matos Mar, "The 'Barriadas' of Lima: An Example of Integration into Urban Life," in Philip M. Hauser, ed., *Urbanization in Latin America,* (Paris: UNESCO, 1961), 170, 175. Compare William Mangin, "Mental Health and Migration to Cities: A Peruvian Case," *Annals of the New York Academy of Sciences,* 84 (1960), 911.

[2]Compare Lisa R. Peattie, *The View from the Barrio,* (Ann Arbor: University of Michigan Press, 1968), 43-44, 47-48.

married by law, and the other half were *unidos*, living in common-law unions. The early drafts of the survey questionnaire contained questions designed to measure the stability of marital unions, but those questions were eliminated when the pilot survey showed them to be offensive to the interviewees. Some sense of the degree of stability can be obtained, however, from an examination of the surnames of the children in the households surveyed. In 59 percent of the households, *all* of the children had the same surname as the current husband of the mother. It would be surprising to find such a phenomenon in a household where a series of husbands had been present to father the woman's children. (A child born of an informal union is considered "illegitimate" under national law, absent some formal recognition by the father. But the child of a union takes the father's name even if the union is informal.) In another 27 percent of the cases, all the children had the surname of the mother. This pattern suggests the absence of a stable marital union but is not conclusive; some such cases may reflect awareness of the national law of legitimacy and recognition.

Apart from the survey, the 1967 study contemplated that the participant-observers living in the barrios would take special note of subjects dropped from the questionnaire because of their sensitivity. The observers reported many statements by men of half-formed intentions to leave their wives but few instances where such an intention was carried into action. Every barrio seems to have its celebrated cases of individuals, both men and women, whose marital turnover rate is high. Many a middle-class Venezuelan thinks of such a case as the barrio norm. But those cases are the subject of gossip within the barrio precisely because they do not fit the usual pattern of barrio family life. The principal motive for moving to a barrio is home ownership, which implies some expectation of family stability.

The Husband's Obligations. This question was asked in the 1967 survey:

> Suppose a man and woman live together, that is, they are *unidos.* How do you think the man should behave? That is, what obligations does the man have to fulfill?

The interviewers were instructed to keep sounding out the respondents, asking, "What else?" Most of the responses were thus multiple, identifying several obligations. By far the most prominent answer, both as a first response (46 %) and taking all responses cumulatively (79 %), was that the husband must bring home money, food, clothes, and the like. The husband's primary obligation, as it is perceived by men and women alike, is to be the breadwinner. This perception is borne out by the figures on contributions to the household's expenses. In the overwhelming majority of cases, the husband who is present in the house provides the chief support for the household. Concern for this obligation to support the wife was expressed indirectly in the answers to a question that seemingly was not related. The questionnaire, in its section on norms of sexual behavior of unmarried young people, asked whether it would be more or less serious for an underage girl to have sexual relations with a boy who is also a minor than it would be if the young man has reached majority. More than seven out of ten respondents answered that the case would be more serious, partly because a boy under age could not be compelled to marry and support the girl.[3]

The two obligations perceived for the husband that share the runner-up position, far behind the duty to support the wife, are these:

> Behave well (be serious, stay home, don't cause scandal, don't get drunk)
>
> Take care of the children, be affectionate to them, discipline them, etc.

Each of these responses was given by about one-third of the interviewees, most frequently in the latter case as a second or third (prompted) response. Fidelity was mentioned by fewer than 3 percent of the respondents and by only 2 out of 239 men. The issue of the husband's sexual fidelity was raised explicitly, however, in a series of questions carefully constructed to avoid asking directly for the respondent's own views. The responses show a considerable intolerance for the husband who brings another woman to live in the same house, but an easing of

---

[3]Of the 11 percent who answered that the case would be less serious, 7 percent appeared to understand the question as calling for a moral judgment, saying that it would be less serious (*menos grave*) for a boy under age, since he would not know what he was doing. Thus, the "more serious" view probably is held even more widely than the seven-out-of-ten figure indicates.

this intolerance in the case of the "other woman" who lives in another barrio. The first of these questions was:

Suppose a man lives in a house with a woman, and that he brings a second woman to live in the same house. What do you think would happen?

The responses to this open-ended question, coded empirically, show some 95 percent believing that the first woman would not accept the situation and only 2 percent believing that she would. In such a situation, 63 percent thought that the neighbors would not continue to visit the house, while 26 percent thought that they would continue to visit. The respondents were further asked whether they thought that the neighbors would have anything to do with the man after such behavior. Fifty-two percent answered negatively and 31 percent affirmatively.

When the situation was altered, so that the man brought the second woman to live in the same barrio but in another house, the responses shifted perceptibly. In this situation, 21 percent of the respondents thought that the first woman would accept the situation,[4] and 72 percent thought she would not. Would the neighbors continue to see the man in such a case? Forty-six percent said "yes," and 39 percent said "no."

When the hypothetical "other woman" was placed in another barrio, 41 percent of all respondents thought the woman would accept the situation,[5] and another 24 percent said, "If she doesn't know about it, it doesn't matter." Only 27 percent responded that the first woman could not accept this situation. The neighbors were expected to react even more charitably; 23 percent (men, 26%; women, 20%) thought the neighbors would stop seeing the man, but 66 percent (men, 62%; women, 68%) said that the neighbors would continue to deal with him.

[4]Of women respondents, 24 percent gave this answer; the figure for men was 16 percent.

[5]Of women respondents, 46 percent gave this answer; the figure for men was 32 percent.

Other obligations of the husband mentioned in the multiple responses to the basic open-ended question were these:

11.9%	Respect the woman
14.4%	Love and affection for the woman, avoid arguments, be nice, don't hit the woman, etc.
5.6%	Marry the woman
21.2%	Educate the children (send them to school)

If the latter response is added to the previously mentioned one about taking care of the children, then about half of the respondents are seen to have expressed the view that a "common-law" husband has obligations toward the children beyond the providing of support for the household. Some interviewees would be counted twice in this process, but it is clear that some obligation toward the children is the second most important one perceived for the husband.

The Wife's Obligations. The 1967 questionnaire posed a similar open-ended question about the obligations of the woman in the same informal-union situation. The coded multiple responses are:

Total Responses	First Responses	
10.8%	7.4%	Same obligations as the man
64.1%	39.0%	Take care of the home, make meals, wash, iron, market, etc.
51.4%	29.0%	Look after the husband, be considerate, etc.
21.0%	9.0%	Respect the husband, obey him, avoid arguments
9.3%	2.8%	Stay home
4.6%	2.1%	Fidelity
44.7%	6.7%	Take care of the children
2.6%	0.8%	Work outside the home if she can
7.7%	3.3%	Other

The obligation mentioned most frequently is something like a reciprocal of the husband's obligation to support the wife and children. One way to read these results would be to conclude that in the barrios material concerns are thought to be the most important in marriage. An alternative possibility is that the word "obligations" carries with it a cold and contractual sound, calling to mind duties of this kind. Also, a barrio, like other communities that are relatively poor, is a place where abstractions are apt to play a role in conversation that is secondary to things that can be seen and touched; the duty to wash and iron, like the duty to bring home dinner, is a duty that is easy to define.

The foregoing responses might be taken to mean that fidelity is not a highly prized virtue in barrio women. However, the participant-observers who lived in barrios all reported that the classical double standard was very much at work there. One observer's report includes several direct quotations from barrio men to the effect that a single sexual transgression by a woman was sufficient ground for abandoning her. (One highly speculative guess would explain the absence of responses about fidelity to the questionnaire's inquiry into the woman's obligations as a reflection of the fact that a wife's infidelity is in some literal sense unthinkable.)

The Effect of Legal Marriage. This question was put to the barrio residents in 1967:

> And if they get married by law, do you think that then the man would have new obligations to fulfill, now that he is legally married? If yes, which?

The response was 68 percent negative. (For the woman's obligations, the answers were 72 percent negative.) The affirmative answers were scattered: more respect for the wife, stay with the wife, be faithful. The most interesting affirmative response was that the man would have the same obligations, "but with greater responsibility." This response was so frequent (about 10%) that it was added to the code for the questionnaire, even though the answer had not been anticipated when the questionnaire was prepared. A person who gives this answer appears to be assuming that the legal system would enforce some marital obligations when the couple are civilly married which would not be enforced when they are living together in an informal union. Both in theory and in practice, that is a dubious assumption. "Common-law" husbands have a legal obligation to support their wives, and a barrio wife's enforcement in court of her support rights is not a realistic expectation whether or not she is legally married.[6]

---

[6]Child support is something else again. See *infra,* pp. 37, 39-40.

In any case, there is no widely shared perception of a duty on the part of a "common-law" husband to marry his wife in a civil or church ceremony. When the respondents answered that it was important to try to persuade young people who were having sexual relations to marry, they were not necessarily talking about a civil marriage or a church marriage but instead seemed to have in mind persuading the couple to set up their own household as husband and wife, with or without a ceremony. Of course, a formal marriage is more prestigious, particularly for the woman.[7]

Termination of Marriage: Child Support, Custody, and Division of Property. In an informal union, of course, there need be no "grounds" for termination of the union. But among the barrio residents who are *unidos,* there is a fairly clear sense of at least some justifications for ending the relationship. While the husband's infidelity appears to be widely tolerated if it is not too blatantly carried on in front of the wife, the standard for the wife is not at all flexible—at least not in the conversation of barrio residents. The most widely accepted "ground" for a wife's decision to terminate an informal union is physical brutality by the husband, either toward the wife or toward her children. Nonsupport appears not to be an independent ground; a man who decides to stop supporting his family ordinarily leaves the household; there is no occasion for the wife to make a decision in such a case.

Upon the termination of an informal union, the children nearly universally stay with the mother or with her family.[8] The notion of an obligation on the departing husband to support his children is not well developed. It will be recalled that in about 40 percent of the cases the children did not all bear the same surname as the resident spouse of the mother. Yet, out of nearly 600 responses, only twenty-six households (4.4%) reported that a non-resident father was contributing anything to the maintenance of the

[7]Peattie, *supra* note 2, at 45, makes the same observation concerning the prestige value of a formal marriage, especially a church marriage.

[8]It is common for the maternal grandmother to take the children under such circumstances and even to keep them when the wife forms another union with a new husband.

household; in 515 cases (86.6%), no one other than those living in the house was contributing.

The most important item of property to be allocated upon the termination of a union is, of course, the house. If the husband has built the house or bought it, then the common practice treats the house as his, to be disposed of as he may choose. The typical case in which the husband is thought to have no such right is the case in which the wife (and perhaps some children by a previous union) had been living in the house when the husband moved in. And even in this case, it is possible to find examples of acquiescence by the wife to the husband's power to control the property. One such case, reported by an observer who was living in a barrio in 1967, was the following: A woman lived in a house with a man and two children from a previous union, aged sixteen and nine. The land on which her house was built had been given to her, and she had paid for the materials and had the house built. The man with whom she was living regularly came home drunk and beat her and her children. She was afraid to leave the children alone in the house for fear of what he might do to them; some of the beatings were administered with a machete. This situation had been in progress for several months. The woman said to the observer that she thought the house was her property but that she did not expect to be able to get the man to leave, even though he was then unemployed and not contributing to the household. The woman assumed that her only remedy was to leave with her children, abandoning the house to the man.[9]

Parent and Child

The barrio population, like the national population of Venezuela, is young. A 1965 estimate placed some 50 percent of Venezuela's population under fifteen years of age and about two-thirds of the population under twenty-five. (In 1965, about 31 percent of the population of the United States was estimated to be under fifteen.) The average barrio household in the 1967 survey included four minors. And a walk through any barrio confirms the impression left by these statistics—children everywhere.

[9]For further discussion of this case, see p. 54, *infra.*

Many of the children are the product of informal unions. In 1961, when the Venezuelan Congress was considering new legislation to protect such children, the draftsmen of the new law reported these national statistics: From 1947 to 1956, the percentage of "illegitimate" births (births outside formal marriage) dropped from 60 percent to 56 percent of the total births in Venezuela. As late as 1969, this figure was conservatively estimated at 53 percent.[10] Since the ratio of informal unions to legal marriages is higher in the barrios than for the nation at large, it seems conservative to assert that well over half the children in the barrios are illegitimate in this formal sense.

Illegitimate birth is seen as a problem in the barrio, but only for the mother who has no man to support her child. Even in such a case, abortion is almost universally (96.1%) rejected as a solution when the issue is presented in the abstract.[11] In fact, contraception is rejected by a large majority (nearly 69%) of both men and women in the barrios surveyed in 1967—similarly in the abstract.

In the barrios, both parents of natural children accept the obligation to care for the children, at least during the time when the parents are living together. But a nonresident father may or may not expect to support his children once he has left the household. One analogue to this latter phenomenon is the absence of any sense of obligation on the part of a man who casually fathers a child by a woman with whom he is not living. The prevailing attitude in this situation appears to be that the mother should expect to support the child herself or with the aid of her family, especially her mother.

Education of the children is high on the list of parental aspirations. But educational opportunity is partly a function of

[10]Asociación Venezolana de Planificación Familiar, Informe . . . ante la Reunión Anual del Consejo Regional y el Comité Médico Regional de la I.P.P.F. 7 (Cuernavaca, Mexico, 1969), cited in Iêda S. Wiarda, *Family Planning Activities in a Democratic Context: The Case of Venezuela* (Columbus, Ohio: Mershon Center, Ohio State University, 1970), at 65, n. 10.

[11]When the issue is presented more concretely, in the context of a woman's real decision whether or not to seek an abortion, the ideal norm reflected in the text apparently breaks down. At the Caracas maternity hospital, in 1964 there was one abortion for every four live births. See Wiarda, *Family Planning Activities,* 103, n. 71. Compare Susan Ann Evans, *Urbanization and Fertility in Latin America: A Comparison of Caracas and Mexico City,* M.A. thesis, (University of California at Los Angeles, 1970), 104. (1.2% of a sample of women in the Caracas maternity hospital admitted to having had an abortion.)

the system of support for the household. If there is no man in the house, even young children may have to work. And even in a barrio that has easy access to a school (thus eliminating the cost of bus fare), sending the children to school implies the expense of dressing them adequately. Despite these obstacles, the barrio children are, on the average, better educated than their parents by a margin of several years of schooling. The husband's perceived obligation to educate the children of an informal union appears to be commonly fulfilled.

The recognition of children by their natural fathers is an explicit goal of national legislative policy. A 1961 law required the directors of public maternity hospitals to encourage a declaration of paternity by the father.[12] The statistics of the 1967 survey tell us that in nearly 60 percent of the barrio households surveyed, all the children carried the surname of the present spouse of the mother. But those figures do not establish that the fathers have formally recognized their natural children. The same law restates the duty of natural parents to support their children. The problem in the case of a non-supporting, nonresident father is one of enforcement; few barrio mothers are able to contemplate a lawsuit, and few are even willing in such a case to seek the aid of the Venezuelan Children's Council (CVN), a government agency whose primary responsibility is child welfare and which is authorized to institute judicial proceedings to compel parents to support their children.

The CVN also is enpowered to intervene in family affairs in cases of child neglect, such as a case in which a mother leaves small children alone for long periods. The final remedy in such a case would be for the CVN to place the children in a foster home or in an institution for children. One of the observers in the 1967 study reported a particularly aggravated case of neglect involving the worst kind of filth and real hunger. When he asked a barrio resident why no action had been taken, this was the response: "The junta won't do anything because [the president] is incompetent, [another officer] is too busy, and the rest don't much care. The neighbors won't because it's too much trouble. Once you report the matter to the Consejo del Niño[CVN], you have

---

[12]*Ley Sobre Protección Familiar, Gaceta Oficial* (Dec. 22, 1961), no. 26, 735, art. 2.

to show up for hearings and trials, and it's too time-consuming." The observer adds this to his report: "I felt there was also the reluctance to act as a 'fink' since they are all poor and don't want to be unfair to a neighbor. Nevertheless, all who knew of the case were shocked by the conditions."

Both the 1967 questionnaire and questions of the participant-observers produced frequent and rather sentimental references to children. The statement quoted earlier about the urge to have a little house to leave to one's children typifies such remarks. The statement is reinforced by the survey's results in the area of inheritance. The barrio resident who owns his house expects to be able to dispose of it upon his death and expects further to leave the house to his family. The questionnaire, however, asked the latter question in an open-ended way. Here are the questions and the responses:

If you died, to whom would you leave your belongings (the house) as inheritance?

70.5%	Children
9.2%	Spouse
8.5%	Children and spouse
9.8%	Other relative
0.3%	Other person
1.6%	Other answer, or don't know

The "natural objects of the bounty" of the barrio resident, then, appear to be children first of all. In the case of a barrio father who leaves the household, this sense of obligation weakens considerably. In the case of the barrio mother, the obligation is strong and enduring.

4. Contractual Relations: The Barrio Credit System

The study dealt in brief compass with the nature of contractual relations in the barrios as reflected in the barrios' credit system. In particular, credit sales and simple cash loans were examined.

In a barrio, a resident seeks credit from a storekeeper because the resident has no money at the time—not because of any "charge-account" convenience factor. Moreover, the existence of an intra-barrio credit system implies a sense of perceived obligation, of trust, of community. Correspondingly, credit relationships within a barrio should increase in importance as time passes, and the study confirms that they did. Even in the older barrios, most people pay cash when they buy from the *bodegas* (small barrio stores); the figure for the study as a whole was 73 percent. (In the two newest barrios, the figures were 89 percent and 85 percent, respectively.) There are marked differences in the residents' expectations of credit in the event of need. In each of the two newest barrios, 44 percent of the respondents answered negatively when asked whether the storekeeper would give them credit if they had no money. In the four oldest barrios, only 28 percent gave a negative answer.

The storekeeper, who sells groceries and minor "general store" items, has only one remedy in the event of continued nonpayment; he can stop giving credit. He cannot count on the barrio junta or the municipal authorities to coerce the debtor into paying. There is no perceived moral obligation on the storekeeper to sell food on credit, although some do give "credit" in the knowledge that they are really doing charity. The storekeeper's criteria for granting credit are what one would expect; if the credit buyer is employed, if he owns his house, if he has a generally good reputation, then he will almost certainly be granted credit, unless he is already in debt to the storekeeper. Some combination of lesser degrees of these factors will justify the granting of credit. A household in which there is no man is kept on a very short credit string—perhaps $6.00 (U.S.) every two weeks.

Since prices are lower in the big markets than in the little barrio bodegas there is a tendency to shop in the markets when cash is available. Another perspective on the same point is that the barrio

42

storekeeper may think it is necessary to give credit in order to maintain his business; it is the very existence of the potential credit relationship that makes the barrio residents want to build up their ties to the storekeeper. The sellers in the big markets, it need hardly be added, do not give credit. Another concern expressed by bodega owners is that resort to the remedy of stopping the credit flow in the event of nonpayment itself carries the risk of making the debtor angry and causing him to refuse to pay what he owes. There is plenty of competition in the barrio. Some 5 percent of all respondents said that they had businesses in the barrios; most of the businesses are bodegas.

Purchases of major items, such as furniture, are normally made outside the barrio and on the basis of installment credit. The price may be borrowed from a bank, but far more frequently it is the seller who gives credit. Employment, rather than the ownership of a house, seems to be the chief criterion for granting installment credit to a barrio resident. The only security for the loan is the purchased item itself. The installment seller does have the force of the national legal system behind him, at least to the extent of repossessing items when payments are not made. For example, the overwhelming majority of buyers of television sets are aware that default in payment will result only in loss of the set. This is, in fact, the installment seller's main remedy; deficiency judgments normally are not sought. The price of the TV set sold on installment payments is high enough for the seller to capture his costs and some profit long before the installments have been completely paid. If only a few payments are left in such a case, the seller may not even bother to go to the expense of repossessing what he has sold. Some barrio residents are aware of this pattern and have taken advantage of it.

About 40 percent of the respondents to the survey had previously borrowed cash in the amount of Bs. 1000 ($220 U.S.) or more. Of the borrowers, over 40 percent obtained their loans from banks; the others borrowed from relatives, friends, or employers. (Although the barrio storekeepers do make small cash loans from time to time, they are not a major source of this type of credit.) These cash loans were only rarely secured; they were normally repaid in installments. The money was borrowed for a variety of purposes: to build or buy a house, to pay medical or funeral expenses, to send money to relatives in need, and even to buy food or consumer goods. While institutional lenders charged interest, private lenders normally did not. Of those who had borrowed Bs. 1000 or more, 95 percent said they had repaid their loans.

Cash loans and consumer credit are characteristics of a community in which the security of transactions rests on a more fundamental underlying stability. Thus, the study's results relating to the barrio credit system support the findings in the areas of housing and family obligations.

5. Security of the Person and Property

Immediately after the fall of Pérez Jiménez, when the barrios consistuted some 40 percent of the total population of Caracas, one of the staples of middle- and upper-class mythology was that the barrios were seething with discontent and were ready to explode. One night—so the fear was commonly expressed—the barrios would empty; their residents would come down out of the hills and sack the city. The results of the study show one major reason why that fear was substantially unfounded; the barrio residents are not very different from the rest of the population in their goals and attitudes. They have come to the barrios in order to own their own houses; they seek employment, education for their children, and community stability. Most importantly, they sense that these expectations are in the process of being realized. Some barrios do have a deserved reputation for being "tough"— although the tendency of the barrio residents is to identify the tough barrio as being the one next to theirs and not their own.

In the first few years after Pérez Jiménez fell, vigilante groups formed in some barrios to enforce order. Those groups have now been disbanded. Their formation shows that the barrio residents insist on order and will provide it for themselves if they consider the police incapable of providing it. The disbanding of the vigilante groups is explained by the residents as a reaction to diminishing need; the police are called when serious trouble occurs, and they respond. Many policemen are themselves barrio residents.

The police are, in fact, rather well regarded in the barrios. The respondents to the survey were asked a general question about their rating of the police; almost half rated the police as "good' or "very good," and only one out of six rated them as "bad" or "very bad." Approval of the police was correlated negatively to the age of the barrio, as noted earlier, with the exception of the youngest barrio still seeking a toehold on its hill in the face of some police harassment. Regardless of the age of the barrio, however, it is the opinion of the barrio residents that the barrios would be more secure if there were more police protection. The question on this subject was open-ended: "What could be done to make the barrio safer?" Two out of three respondents answered this question, without prompting, by saying that more police vigilance was needed. (Here again, the ratio was much lower in the newest barrio—two out of five.) Since the disappearance of the vigilante groups, no new intra-barrio security system has emerged. The barrio junta does not normally offer protection of the person, even in the form of punishment of offenders.[1] What the junta will do is call the police, who are seen as the natural protectors of physical security in the barrio.

Nine out of ten of the survey's respondents reported that neither they nor members of their families had been involved in fights. The few fights that were reported more frequently involved men and boys and only rarely involved women. Alcohol appears to be the most significant immediate cause of violence, although there is some reason to believe that drinking merely releases violence that has deeper causes. One murder that occurred in a barrio where one of the participant-observers was living was the result of a long-standing grudge. Family feuds are not unknown, but more typically result in nothing more violent than the dumping of trash or fights among teen-age boys.

A frequent complaint of barrio residents concerns the presence of juvenile gangs. This complaint is heard least of all in the newest barrios and most frequently in the oldest ones. This pattern reflects general attitudes toward physical security in the barrios; the older the barrio, the less secure the residents feel in their persons. The gangs do exist, especially in the older and more centrally located barrios. But most of their activity is harmless social activity. They appear to bother other barrio residents chiefly because of their noise and their disrespectfulness. They may become involved in some feuding, but they do not terrorize the barrios.

A second murder in a barrio where another of the participant-observers lived was the result of a nighttime robbery. The barrio was old and close to the center of the city, and it had a reputation for being "tough." The reputation appears to date from the period immediately following the fall of Pérez Jiménez, when this barrio was the scene of frequent clashes between residents and the police. The residents found the murder shocking, but the incident's

[1]See Chapter 6, *infra.*

46

property-crime aspect was not unusual. In the barrios that are located near the center of the old city, theft is not uncommon.

Three-quarters of all the barrio residents surveyed, however, said that they had not had anything stolen from them in the barrios. This figure cannot merely represent the barrios' poverty, for nearly every family has something that might be stolen: a watch, a transistor radio, a camera. Rather, the low number of residents who report having been victimized seems related to other characteristics of the barrios: high level of employment, home ownership, family stability. The small barrio stores are natural targets for theft, and in fact their owners do report more thefts than do other residents. In some cases, the owner of a bodega may even think he knows who has stolen from him, but say that he fears to report the thief to the police because of possible retaliation. One storekeeper who had been repeatedly victimized had taken to sleeping in his store to protect it.

Only 19 percent of the barrio residents felt that they had been cheated by sellers of goods. Of those few who said they had been cheated, only one out of nine had made any complaint to authorities; all the rest either complained to the seller or did nothing. The interviewees were also asked, hypothetically, what they would do if they had a dispute over a question of commercial fraud: "To whom would you go to solve the problem?" Some 41 percent said that they would do nothing or would merely complain to the seller. Of the 52 percent who said they would go to the authorities, a substantial majority (30%) named the police; the other authorities mentioned were the municipal council (11%), the courts (6%), the market authorities (4%) and even the barrio junta (1%). Thus, the police are seen as the principal resort in cases of fraud, as well as in cases of personal injury. In cases of simple theft, also, a majority of respondents say they would go to the police. But of the persons who had actually been the victims of theft, only one-quarter had in fact complained to the police or other authorities. The police are thus a source of security in the sense in which security is a state of mind. They are a potential resort primarily and an actual resort more rarely.

6. The Junta

Formation; Patterns of Cooperation

In most of the barrios of Caracas (and in nine of the twelve barrios studied) there are community leadership groups called juntas. These groups act to organize cooperative work projects and also perform some rule-making and dispute-settling functions. The junta typically comes into existence at the time the barrio is formed; its members are either the organizers of the invasion that establishes the barrio or a committee of the earliest settlers. In either case, the junta's first job is apt to be consolidation of the barrio's existence, which means, above all, defense against the police. This defense is carried on by a variety of means, the most important of which is political.[1] The junta seeks out a member of the city council or some other official who may be friendly and persuades him to get municipal approval of the occupation of the land. The approval usually is given in an informal way; the word is passed to the police not to interfere with the occupation of the land by the new residents, the the barrio begins to receive public aid in the construction of improvements. This aid may take the form of government provision of water lines and sewers, or it may simply involve the provision of materials such as concrete for the construction of stairways. Whatever the form, once the aid is given, would-be claimants to the land, public or private, know that their claims are unlikely to prevail.

The public-works function is, in fact, the most important one the junta performs. Not only does the junta represent the barrio to the government and other outside agencies; it also organizes the barrio residents for work projects. Those who do not work are expected to make small cash contributions toward the community's projects, and the junta collects these "voluntary" payments. Typically, the junta will organize a small project, such as the grading and paving of a road or the laying of water pipes.

---

[1]For analysis of the barrio junta's connections with the national political parties, see Talton Ray, *The Politics of the Barrios of Venezuela,* (Berkeley: University of California Press, 1969), chapters 6 and 7.

Such a project is manageable in a short period of time, and its benefits are easily understood. Absent either one of these favorable factors, the project is unlikely to succeed.

In dealing with the government agencies that provide such things as building materials, the junta is aided substantially if its leaders are agents of the right political parties. (The governmental structure in Caracas is sufficiently complex that different parties may have independent capacity to aid a barrio.[2]). This phenomenon, not unknown in the history of certain large cities in the United States, results in a high correlation between the degree of activity by the junta and its intensity of political orientation. In one very large barrio studied, all the members of the junta said when interviewed that politics had nothing to do with the way the junta operated. However, all but one of them were members of Acción Democrática (then in control of the Presidency and of the government of the Federal District, which includes the portion of Caracas where the barrio was located), and the junta's president was on the payroll of the Ministry of Public Works.

There is no Venezuelan statute prescribing a method for electing members of a barrio junta or for fixing the junta's term of office. Some juntas are associated with regional or national associations (which, in turn, are arms of national political parties) and thus may adopt the model constitutions published by the associations. But in most barrios, elections are held irregularly, principally to fill vacancies in the office of president. Many barrio residents, and even members of the junta, assume that the period of a junta's term is one or two years. In practice, however, a successful junta—and that means a successful president—will hold office for a longer time.[3] The president may resign because he becomes too occupied with his non-barrio job or because of ill health; more typically, he will resign because he is tired of being president or because his popularity has decreased. An unsuccessful president may resign after only a few months in office.

---

[2]See generally David J. Myers, *The Political Process of Urban Development: Caracas under Acción Democrática*, (Ann Arbor: University Microfilms, 1969).

[3]The barrios studied did not evidence the *caciquismo* (strong, autocratic, informal, personalist leadership, often resting on the threat of violence) noted by Ray, *supra* note 1, at 59. Compare Wayne Cornelius, "A Structural Analysis of Urban Caciquismo in Mexico," *Urban Anthropology*, 1 (Fall, 1972), 234.

"Successful," in this context, means able to accomplish the junta's goals, primarily in the field of public works. Thus, the cooperation of a government agency may be crucial to the junta's continuation in office. At least as important to the junta's success is its ability to convince the barrio's residents that they should join in cooperative projects. The judgment of nearly all writers on marginal squatter settlements in Latin America is that this cooperation is easier to secure in the more recently settled barrios and becomes harder as the barrio gets older, more prosperous, and more integrated into the city.[4] The Caracas study confirms this thesis.

Occasionally it is suggested that the barrio residents' early inclination toward cooperation is a remnant of rural or small-town patterns of cooperative work. That is a plausible explanation— although we have seen that most barrio residents have lived in the city for a time before coming to their present homes. But other explanations may also be valid. The very newness of a venture instills an optimistic, cooperative frame of mind. Most barrio residents, we have seen, come there with the expectation of something better than what they have left behind. The new ranchos are not the refuge of the desperate, but symbols of hope. Furthermore, the residents must come together at the outset for purposes of defense or consolidation. As the barrio becomes established, the residents are, at the same time, strengthening their ties to the world outside, so they are more inclined to take a "what's-in-it-for-me" position when asked to cooperate. Talton Ray notes that no one seems to himself to be so foolish as a barrio resident who works alone on a community project while his neighbors are watching.[5] Still another explanation emphasizes this latter theme. During the early years of a barrio, the gains to be realized by an individual barrio resident or his family through cooperative labor are readily apparent, as in the building of a staircase, or improvement of the water supply or sewage facilities. As the barrio grows older and the basic improvements have been made, it is more difficult for any individual barrio resident to see what benefit will accrue to him or his family by his

---

[4]For example, William Mangin, "Mental Health and Migration to Cities: A Peruvian Case," *Annals of the New York Academy of Sciences,* 84 (1960), 911, 914.

[5]Ray, *supra* note 1, at 79.

working on a community project. In these terms, cooperation does not imply a sense of community; rather, it is based upon self-interest. It is nevertheless true that during the earlier period at least, the aggregation of self-interests produces cooperation.

The residents of the newer barrios almost all know that a junta exists. In the older barrios, greater numbers of residents are ignorant of the existence of a junta; even those who do know of the junta tend to characterize it as "inactive" or "not very active." And yet even in the older barrios, cooperation remains the pattern among the residents, at least in the sense that they say cooperation is a good idea. In response to an open-ended question in the survey ("What do you think a resident of a barrio should do to improve it?), some 62 percent answered that one should cooperate, unite, etc. (About 6.5 percent answered, "Nothing.") The positive answers were in a lower proportion in the older barrios and, curiously, in the newest of all. Perhaps during the very first months of this barrio's existence, everyone was so busy getting his own house constructed that he had not yet identified community needs that demanded cooperation. Some 25 percent of the residents of this new barrio answered to the above question, "Let everyone work (build) on his own account; let everyone leave others alone, etc." The average percentage for this answer in all the barrios surveyed was 14 percent.

Just under a third (31%) of the interviewees said that they (or their husbands or wives) would accept a position in the junta if it were offered. Of the 62 percent who answered negatively to this question, some 38 percent thought it necessary to volunteer a reason for declining: "I don't have time," or "I am too old," or "I can't read." While only 3 percent were willing to say that residents of the barrio should not cooperate with the junta, more than one-quarter reported that they had not, in fact, ever cooperated. While these figures do not form an entirely consistent pattern, it seems fair to say that cooperation with the junta is widely considered to be appropriate, at least in the abstract; the extent to which community cooperation is generally accepted as a personal obligation among the barrio residents is less clear. The residents of all barrios generally approved the activities of the existing juntas. While 62 percent answered that the juntas' activities had been "very good" or "good" for the barrios, only 4.5 percent said that the juntas had been "bad" or "very bad."

In the larger barrios, sectionalism is a persistent problem. The barrio junta tends to be dominated by the residents of the older sectors located nearest the city streets. The people on top of the hill feel left out of the barrio's community activities and excluded from the benefit of cooperative projects, and with good reason. They *are* left out. At the time of the 1967 study, these feelings were crystallizing in some barrios, producing new and separate juntas and even the adoption of new names to identify barrios that were emerging in these excluded sectors. One of the participant-observers lived in the upper portion of a barrio called La Charneca. While he was there, the residents of his zone established a new junta for a barrio which they named not Alta Charneca but Colinas de las Acacias. Las Acacias is the name of an upper-middle-class urbanization on the other side of the hill. The idea behind the new name was not so much to identify the hilltop barrio with Las Acacias as it was to emphasize its independence from La Charneca. La Charneca is an old barrio whose lower portions are practically indistinguishable from the rest of the city. The junta in La Charneca has become little more than a political club. The barrio has a reputation as a high-crime area. On the top of the hill, though, there is now a new barrio with a new junta; community cooperation is the order of the day.

Lawmaking and Dispute Resolution

If the junta's public-works activities can be characterized as executive functions, the junta also has some functions that can be called legislative and judicial. The preceding chapters on rights in land and family obligations have described some of the reach of the junta's power and some of its limitations. The most important legislative functions of the junta relate to rights in land. The junta, immediately after it is organized, assumes the power to measure and designate parcels of land to be occupied by newly arriving residents. Even after the barrio is well established, new residents are added, either building on unoccupied parcels or acquiring already built houses by purchase or rental. The junta may seek to control new building, but it does not decide whether a new arrival can buy or rent an existing house. Any effort to enforce such a decision would be regarded as an unwarranted interference with the property rights of the seller or landlord. The exception to this pattern, as we have noted before, is the case of the illegal rental of a rancho. A strong junta will intervene in such a case, not to prevent the tenant from occupying but to prevent the landlord from evicting the tenant for nonpayment of rent.

Another law-making function, closely related to the public-works responsibilities of the junta, is the designation of places for the barrio residents to deposit trash and garbage. This is not a trivial matter; certainly no one who lives in a barrio thinks of trash disposal as a minor problem. Here, as in the designation of lots for new residents to occupy, the legislative function of the junta blends into its dispute-resolving function. Disputes about trash disposal can be of long duration, since each day produces its own new opportunities for trouble; in contrast, a boundary dispute is normally settled once and for all.

The foregoing discussion suggests that much of the junta's law-making is accomplished in its handling of particular cases that come before it for action. That suggestion is not misleading. Most of what might be called the barrios' distinctive contribution to their own legal system (that is, the portions of the effective law governing the barrios that do not derive directly from the national legal system) is remarkably similar to the development of Anglo-American common law. Thus, when the junta does make law, it normally does so case by case. While these "judicial" decisions are not recorded formally—most juntas keep only the most sketchy records—nonetheless precedents are remembered. Even the most general conversation with a member of a junta about the norms enforced by the junta is sure to call up illustrative examples of previous cases.

The dispute-resolving functions of the junta vary from barrio to barrio in positive correlation to the junta's strength and level of activity in promoting community cooperation. A junta that is not organizing road-building or other public-works activities is not likely to try to resolve individual disputes, nor would such a junta's decisions be respected.

Even in an active junta, the junta's adjudicatory power is typically limited to two kinds of controversies. The first is that of disputes over land, of which the clearest case is that of the boundary dispute. But other claims based on rights in land are also frequently brought before the junta.[6]

[6]Despite the junta's important role in settling land-related disputes, however, only 14 percent of the respondents named the junta as their expected resort in the event of a dispute over the right to build on a parcel of land or to live in a particular house. In contrast, 48 percent named various governmental authorities as their potential resort in such a case.

The second category is that of behavior of individuals which seriously disturbs the peace of the barrio. Thus, the junta will normally not intervene in family quarrels. In the case, discussed in Chapter 3, of the woman whose husband was beating her and her children, the woman presumably was entitled to protection by some agency, even a court. But her only *effective* remedy would have been to go to the junta, and she knew they would not intervene. However, in a few cases of family squabbles, a strong junta will take action. Those relatively rare cases usually involve disturbance of the neighbors. Thus, if a husband and wife quarrel in such a way as to become a nuisance (in both the legal and the popular sense), the junta may order them out of the barrio. Even if they owned their house, such an order would be effective, for the municipal council would not interfere with the junta's decision, absent some special influence on behalf of the excluded persons.

So, too, the junta usually will not offer protection in the case of theft or physical assault. Crimes such as these are regarded as the jurisdiction of the police, even in relatively isolated barrios. Often, of course, the junta will be the agency that calls the police, and there is some reason to believe that the police are more ready to respond to such a call than they might be if they were called by someone else. During the period of greatest influx into Caracas just after the fall of Pérez Jiménez, some juntas organized vigilante committees, but practically all of those groups are now defunct. However, persistent troublemakers who engage in fights or in open violation of the prevailing moral code may be ordered out of the barrio. This sanction, however, is very rarely invoked and not at all in barrios where the residents have legal title to their land.

What emerges then from this description of the barrio junta's dispute-resolving functions? We believe, consistent with our earlier expressed conclusion, that this function can properly be called an adjudicatory one—a typical feature of a system of law. The junta does not appear to choose or decide its cases on an ad hoc basis. Rather, its jurisdiction seems relatively narrow and well-defined. Its continuing authority derives from an acceptance by the community of its decisions as conforming with established principles and their expectations. In short, we think this demonstrates that the junta exercises a judicial function, properly so called.

Sometimes it is hard for a resident to reach his house without passing over the lot of another resident . . . the matter may be resolved by the building of a common concrete stairway.

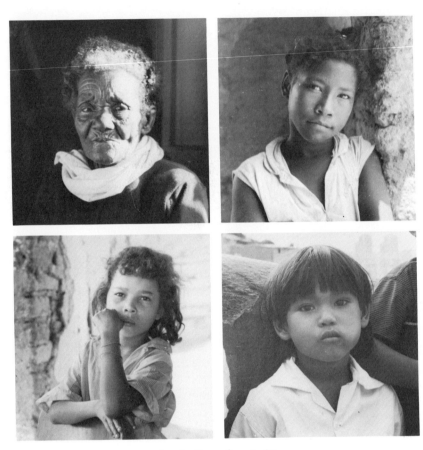

A selection of portraits.

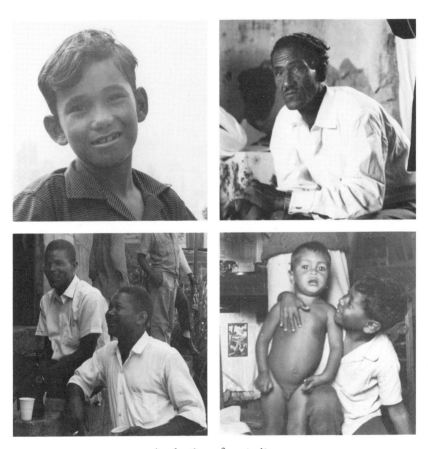

A selection of portraits.

Sunday afternoon: leisure time on the barrio summit.

The overwhelming majority of the barrios occupy hillsides.

Sunday afternoon: marbles . . . and bolas criollas.

Most of the businesses in the barrio are bodegas.

The homes in the barrio vary greatly.

In 1990, the best estimates are that Caracas will be a city of 3.5 to
4 million inhabitants. The Valley, of course, does not get any bigger.

In the barrio, there are many little stores that sell basic food items.

The great majority of the barrio residents in Caracas have lived for a time in the city before moving to the barrio, and thus are not rural migrants when they come to the barrio.

Children can play anywhere . . . The woman's duty to wash and iron
is easy to define.

7. Patterns of Change in the Barrios

The barrios surveyed were selected so that they could be compared on the basis of age. The oldest barrios had been founded in the 1920s; the newest one was only five months old at the time of the survey. It had been expected that there would be significant differences among the barrio residents according to the ages of the barrios in which they lived; the survey validated that assumption.[1]

It has been noted that the principal motivation for moving to a barrio is the opportunity for home ownership. In the newest barrio everyone owns his own house; in the newer barrios generally, 98 percent either own their own houses or live in relatives' houses. The percentage of ownership decreases to 66 percent in the older barrios. At the same time, the uncertainty of *land* ownership decreases in the older barrios; the greatest percentage of owners of land is in three of the four oldest barrios. Thus, more people are renters in the oldest barrios, but those who do own their houses are also more likely to own the land.

These patterns of ownership are reflected in the investments of the barrio residents in housing. The youngest barrios are composed of shacks with walls made of wood or of cardboard cartons and roofs of zinc. But after only a few years of existence, a barrio changes its appearance. Houses take on a more permanent look as concrete walls and roofs are added, followed by stucco and paint.[2] Such a consistent record of investment would be possible only in communities with a sense of security of tenure.

In the barrio residents' commercial dealings, there are noticeable differences that are related to barrio age. For example,

[1]The age of the head of the family correlated positively with the age of the barrio. Thus, the older barrios are populated by older people. In the newest barrios, for example, 34 percent of heads of families were under thirty, and 12 percent were over fifty. In the oldest barrios, 17 percent of heads of families were under thirty, and 26 percent were over fifty. See Appendix C for questionnaire responses that furnish data for the discussion in this section.

[2]In the Oficina Ministerial del Transporte, where an elaborate survey of the city has been carried out in preparation for the construction of the Caracas subway, a series of maps depicts the growth of the barrios in various eras during the twentieth century. These maps also show certain areas which formerly were classified as barrios but which have since lost that designation as the areas have blended into the city.

for the barrios as a whole, 58 percent of the residents buy all their food outside the barrio (where prices are lower); 7 percent buy food both inside and outside, and 35 percent buy it exclusively inside. In the newest barrios, 73 percent buy their food *outside* the barrio. In the oldest barrios, the comparable figure is 40 percent. One explanation, of course, is that it takes some time for businesses to become established in a new barrio and that progressively more bodegas are opened as time passes. Even however, in the barrio that was only 5 months old, there was a bodega. Another explanation for the greater use of non-barrio markets is that most new arrivals in a barrio—especially a new barrio—have come from other parts of the city and are familiar with shopping opportunities in the city.

Credit relationships in the barrio also develop over time; the older the barrio, the greater the percentage of residents who have received credit from the bodega. Furthermore, in the older barrios more residents expect to be given credit if they should need it.

Incomes in the newest barrios were the lowest of all. The highest incomes, however, were not found in the oldest barrios but rather in the middle group of barrios arranged according to age. This datum raises the possibility that as the barrios grow older and become integrated into the city, they tend to become more like traditional center-city slums, which are at best static in their poverty and at worst continuing to decay.

The evidence on this score is conflicting. Supporting the urban slum model is that fact that the greatest number and proportion of renters, as distinguished from home-owners, live in the oldest barrios. And rental, rather than ownership, is a prime characteristic of an urban slum. On the other hand, the skill level of the barrio residents' employment continues to rise with age of the barrio, as does the educational level of the children, although this may be due to the greater age of the children in the older barrios. So, too, the physical condition of the houses of the oldest barrios and the general socio-economic characteristics of the residents are at a level above that associated with traditional urban slums.

An issue that may be different from the future of the barrios themselves is that of the future of the residents. There is good reason to believe that they are in the process of raising their own socio-economic status over time. Thus, whereas practically all of the houses in the youngest barrios were owned by the residents or their relatives, about one-third of the houses in the oldest barrios were owned by others, suggesting that the landlords had achieved a higher economic level. And half of these rentals were owned by persons living outside of the barrios, suggesting that they had achieved an economic level that permitted them to move out, while retaining an investment in housing in the barrio.

Interestingly, there is no significant age-of-barrio difference in the area of family obligations.[3] This stability of response suggests that these attitudes and relationships are deeply rooted and are not significantly affected by changes in the immediate environment.

There are differences between the older and newer barrios with respect to the security of person and property. The lowest theft rate appears in the newest barrios. The highest tendency toward property crime, however, does not appear in the oldest barrios but rather in the barrios that are most centrally located. Fights are uncommon in all the barrios, although the problem of juvenile gangs is perceived as more serious in the older barrios. There is greatest hostility to the police in some of the oldest barrios and a more receptive attitude toward the police in the younger barrios. The one exception to the latter pattern is the newest barrio, where many of the residents are still struggling against the police to establish their residence. Community cooperation is, as has been noted, at its highest levels during the early days of a barrio's existence; as the barrio grows older, the junta loses prestige and power. It is easy to understand why cooperation is the norm at the outset; the barrio residents typically need to cooperate in order to defend the barrio's very existence and to use the political system to secure such consolidating public services as a water supply, electric power, roads and sewers. Cooperative work projects, often associated with the providing of these services, attract labor and financial support easily during the barrio's early days. As time passes, there is a tendency for the residents' ties to the world outside to become firmer, so that they are more likely to insist on some short-range return for any work they perform for the community.[4]

---

[3]There is a slightly greater tolerance for the "other woman" situation in the older barrios. Also, in the older barrios there is a greater acceptance of the desirability of preventing the birth of a child to a girl who is not living in a stable union.

[4]See pp. 50-51, *supra*.

The differences among barrios related to barrio age thus suggest, in the aggregate, a process of change that is characterized by physical improvements, the development of intra-barrio economic relations, increasing employment and income levels, increasing educational levels, and an eventual falling-off of community cooperation that is directly related to the achievement of the barrio's basic community needs and the simultaneous integration of the residents into the life of the city.

8. Law and Participatory Development in the Barrios

The growth of the barrios in and around Venezuela's major cities is perhaps visualized more easily as a result of development rather than as a cause. The barrios are thus seen as part of larger processes bearing grander labels: urbanization, industrialization. But the barrio has its own internal dynamics which serve to condition the activities of its residents. Furthermore, the day-to-day decisions of the people of the barrios, in the aggregate, may be of importance even to public and private developmental decision-makers at the highest levels. The cabinet minister responsible for housing cannot sensibly ignore those individual decisions by barrio residents which, taken as a whole, constitute a major portion of what his statistics will call "housing investment." And when the Avon lady knocks at the doors of barrio houses, the reason is that each individual barrio woman is part of what someone has characterized as a "market."

At least as investors and consumers, the barrio residents are integrated into the economic life of the world outside the barrios. But their integration goes well beyond the economic sphere. Not only do barrio residents work and shop and borrow money outside the barrios; they also read newspapers and watch television, discuss politics, and seek to make government respond to their community needs. They are favorably disposed toward the police and do not hesitate to call for police aid in time of trouble. They know something of national law, from the rule forbidding the rental of ranchos, to the inheritance rights of a recognized child, to the critical ages in a case of statutory rape.

The integration of the barrio dwellers into the value system of the city and nation is also indicated by another set of characteristics denoting a high level of stability among the residents. Families move to the barrios *as* families, for the purpose of owning their own homes. Husbands and wives live together in stable unions; the husband is normally employed and is expected to support the household; the children bear his name. The children go to school, and education is almost universally regarded as a means of advancement. The barrio house is usually owned by someone in the family; ownership implies the expectation of quiet enjoyment of the house and the further expectation of compensation if the occupancy is disturbed, such as by a government taking of the land; the barrio junta will protect the house owner against a considerable variety of potential internal interferences with his quiet enjoyment. This security of expectations is based on a long tenure history; in the oldest barrios, nearly half the heads of families have lived in the same houses for more than ten years. Major improvements are regularly made to barrio houses, to the point that one can tell the approximate age of a barrio merely by looking at it. As the barrio becomes established, not only do concrete walls replace packing-boxes; other kinds of institution-building go on as well, such as the formation of some lasting credit arrangements, the regularized resolution of land disputes, and cooperative public-works activities. The junta eventually declines in importance, but normally only after having accomplished its main purposes.

Families who share these characteristics—by far the majority of barrio families—are scarcely living in the traditional urban slum, where the main road to betterment is the road that leads to some other place. Barrio life is not glamorous; these are relatively poor communities that have major problems. But by any test, the barrio residents are not those alienated, normless hordes which populate middle-class myth in Caracas.[1] Instead, the picture of the barrio drawn in this study emphasizes stability, integration, and orderly progress.

The law of the barrio is both a result and a cause of these phenomena of orderly progress. If the move to the barrio, for example, is motivated by the desire for home ownership, then it is not surprising that a junta is typically organized immediately upon the initial formation of the barrio and charged with the primary responsibility of protecting the new residents' tenure against both external and internal threats. Thus change begets rules and institutions of the kind that we have termed "law." In turn, the

[1]Even so careful a study as the CENDES study of conflict and consensus began by taking as an a priori hypothesis that the cultural characteristics of barrio dwellers could be epitomized thus: "Low level of education and a traditional style of evaluation but high exposure to mass media and high aspirations; 'uprooted,' no sense of belonging to the communities where they now live, ties to the places of origin lost." Frank Bonilla and José Silva Michelena, eds., *A Strategy for Research on Social Policy,* (Cambridge, Mass.: M.I.T. Press, 1967), 41.

successful defense of the residents' land tenure leads to a continuous process of investment in barrio housing. Thus law can beget change.

These are grand themes: the reactions of law to change in its environment, and the role of law in retarding, promoting, and guiding such change. The type of change with which we are here concerned is that of "development."

We use the term in the sense of improvement of the standard of living with respect to both the material side of life and integration of the developing unit with the larger society. There is an implicit value assumption here; that is, that these improvements are to be desired. Whatever our own views on this issue, it is clear that those who live in the barrios seek these ends. Our concern here is to explicate the relationship between law and development. For this purpose, the interactions of law and development can be illustrated by the microcosm of the barrios of Caracas.

Economists, especially economic planners, frequently complain that the law, with its rigidities and formalities, is an obstacle to development. The complaint is often justified, for much of law is the embodiment of tradition, a bulwark against the forces of change. In the context of the barrios, a thorough-going enforcement of property rights would prevent the formation of a new barrio; squatters would barely have time to squat before being removed.

Once the barrio is established, by means however unlawful, the residents themselves begin to organize, to rely upon law.[2] The barrios' system of law, aided by governmental action that did not relate to legal titles to land, has produced the security that has turned shacks into concrete-block houses, in the classical pattern outlined by Bentham,[3] Weber,[4] and Commons.[5] The constant, incremental improvement of barrio housing by the residents

[2] For a discussion of one squatters' organization in Wisconsin, relating the organization to broader themes of development, see J. Willard Hurst, *Law and the Conditions of Freedom in the Nineteenth-Century United States,* (Madison: University of Wisconsin Press, 1956), 3-6.

[3] Jeremy Bentham, *Theory of Legislation,* Trans. by R. Hildreth from Etienne Dumont (London: Truebner, 1871).

[4] Max Rheinstein, ed., *Max Weber on Law in Economy and Society,* (Cambridge, Mass.: Harvard University Press, 1954).

[5] John Commons, *The Legal Foundations of Capitalism,* (New York: Macmillan Co., 1924).

themselves rests on the system of rights, immunities, and obligations that in the aggregate result in security of tenure.

There are, of course, different ways of achieving those goals previously described in our definition of "development." Most of the current literature on economic growth—and development is manifestly more than increases in per capita production—emphasizes the importance of social and institutional factors in producing economic development.[6] The model of development found in the barrios is that of *participatory development*—developmental activity by large numbers of people at the lower levels of the society and economy.[7] This model implies a redefinition of personal and group goals: a sense of destiny control, a concern for achievement, a willingness to take moderate risks, a concern for the common good, a sense of participation.[8]

A very different approach to development—an approach that failed in Caracas itself—was the Venezuelan government's construction of the fifteen-story *superbloques* to house families who were driven out of barrio homes, which were then razed. This policy, which hastened the downfall of the Pérez Jiménez regime, did not merely de-emphasize participatory development but directly attacked it. In contrast, the barrio-improvement aspects of the Emergency Plan of 1958, although part of a national governmental policy, emphasized the virtues of participatory development and (not so incidentally) capitalized on popular hostility to the razing of barrios.

The barrio resident who builds and improves his own home, unlike the head of a family who is handed the key to an apartment in a *superbloque*, takes some risk, achieves, gains confidence in his

[6]The literature is enormous and is experiencing a high growth rate. We cite only two works, both by economists and both giving great weight to what used to be called non-economic factors in economic development. Everett E. Hagen, *On the Theory of Social Change: How Economic Growth Begins*, (Homewood, Ill.: The Dorsey Press, 1962); Gunnar Myrdal, *Asian Drama*, (New York: Pantheon, 1968).

[7]*But compare* W. Arthur Lewis, *The Theory of Economic Growth*, (London: Allen and Unwin, 1955), 264-265.

[8]See, e.g., David C. McClelland, *The Achieving Society*, (Princeton, N.J.: Van Nostrand, 1961); Albert O. Hirschman, *Development Projects Observed*, (Washington: Brookings Institution, 1967); William F. Whyte and Lawrence K. Williams, *Toward an Integrated Theory of Development: Economic and Noneconomic Variables in Rural Development*, (Ithaca: Cornell University, 1968); Myron Weiner, ed., *Modernization: The Dynamics of Growth*, (New York: Basic Books, 1966); and the works cited in note 6, *supra*—plus, of course, Lewis, *supra* note 7.

74

control over the future, becomes interested in community development projects, and gains a stake in a system that he has made to work in his own interest. The reinforcement of a development mentality is particularly effective in the context of home improvement, which has an immediate and obvious payoff.[9] Thus the law of the barrios produces tenure security conducive to the residents' investment in their own housing through activities that contribute to the reconstruction of the actors' attitudes, thus generating further participatory development.

The precise ways in which law plays a role in this process of participatory development are complex. A legal system may coerce (as when the barrio junta keeps one neighbor from encroaching on another's parcel of land); it may reward (for example, by protecting the house owner's tenure, permitting him to enjoy the fruits of his labor); and it may facilitate (as when the junta organizes a cooperative drainage project to prevent rainwater from undermining houses in the barrio). Each of these functions of law also performs an educational function, changing the barrio resident's view of what is possible for him to do. The law can work to change the resident's view of the surrounding situation by working to change the situation itself. The law can also work to change the barrio resident's image of himself.

The barrios are fertile ground for the production of a development-oriented self-image on the part of the residents. The barrio resident is apt to be "urban" in his outlook, even if he does prefer a small house to an apartment in a tower. Half of the barrio residents have grown up in a city, and most migrants to the barrios have had substantial previous urban experience. The move to the barrio itself is indicative of several important characteristics of the new resident. He is an innovator by definition, and since "mere survival is a feat for the innovator,"[10] the successful move reinforces his inclination toward innovation. He has moved to the barrio in order to improve the lot of his family, demonstrating that he already has a rational/instrumental view of the world rather than a fatalistic

---

[9]See Whyte and Williams, *supra* note 8, at 68.

[10]Hirschman, *supra* note 8, at 27.

75

view. Although the barrio resident may share some of the traditional peasant suspicions,[11] he is not suspicious of the idea of mobility and self-improvement. His aspirations are high.[12] The migrant's motivation to own a house indicates at least some interest in the acquisition of things, which presumably will continue to motivate him to work and to save. And since the barrio resident tends to be employed, he is producing an income that provides some surplus for saving and investment.[13]

If the barrio resident tends to come equipped with a set of attitudes and perceptions that are favorable to his participation in the development process, it is also true that the barrio's setting tends to reinforce that mentality. It would be extraordinary if the influence of law in the barrios were unwaveringly favorable to development; it is not. The multifold interactions of legal institutions and development in the barrios can only be illustrated here.

The Resident's Perception of "The Situation"

Fatalism Versus Rationality. The move to the barrio itself implies a sense of control over one's destiny, a sense that the world can be manipulated through rational effort. The security of tenure that encourages housing investment also promotes the investor's sense that the world responds to effort, as does the barrio junta's organization of modest public-works projects.

The Concept of Limited Good. Since development, even participatory development, depends not only on individual effort in a competitive situation but also on some form of cooperation, it is vital to lay to rest the "static pie" mentality which assumes that one man's advancement necessarily implies another's loss. This sort of perception, sometimes associated with peasants,

---

[11]See Talton Ray, *The Politics of the Barrios of Venezuela,* (Berkeley: University of California Press, 1969), 70-78, for a pessimistic view of barrio residents' willingness to join cooperative work and an explanation based on a suspiciousness that comes from insecurity. Our findings are inconsistent with Ray's statements of fact, and our explanations are correspondingly more optimistic.

[12]Bonilla and Silva Michelena, *supra* note 1, at 41.

[13]Whyte and Williams, *supra* note 8, at 69:
    Concepts of storage and delayed gratification are not readily grasped and acted upon in situations where scarcity prevails.

is antithetical to attitudes that are "modern."[14] The almost universal pattern of organization of a junta immediately upon the formation of a new barrio shows that the barrio residents do value cooperation; the survey confirms the assumption. What is critical for the preservation of these attitudes is some success for the junta in the first years of the barrio's existence. If the junta is able to deliver a new road or a water system, it will also be able to exercise jurisdiction to resolve certain conflicts. In the latter "judicial" situation, of course, frequently one man's gain is another's loss; yet the loser knows that he gains in a more general way, for the junta can also be counted on to protect him in an appropriate case in the future.

Trusting Others. The degree to which others can be trusted most obviously affects developmental decision-making that depends on cooperation, but it is also important to a variety of development-oriented activities by individuals acting on their own account in competitive market situations. The barrio credit system rests on trust,[15] since there is no security either for the storekeeper's advances of credit or for the typical intra-barrio cash loan. These credit relationships increase as time passes, because neighbors become better acquainted and more able to trust one another. One of the ways in which the residents come to have experiences that reinforce their mutual trust is through participation in cooperative work for the community's benefit and through mutual aid in the construction of houses. The junta plays a critical role in persuading people to cooperate. And the government's delivery of building materials at a strategic moment may serve not only to get a community project completed, but also to enhance the residents' inclination to work with each other and to trust each other. If market-oriented development requires the "depolarization of economic relations" and "learning to deal fairly with strangers,"[16] then it is vital that there be a base on which to rest confidence and trust. In the barrios, legal institutions provide that base.

[14]See Everett M. Rogers, *Modernization Among Peasants: The Impact of Communication,* (New York: Holt, Rinehart and Winston, 1969), 28-29.

[15]The Spanish word for the process of advancing credit is *fiar,* to trust.

[16]Kenneth H. Parsons, "Institutional Aspects of Agricultural Development Policy," *Journal of Farm Economics,* 48 (Dec., 1966), 1185, 1189.

The Benevolence or Malevolence of Governmental Authority.
One aspect of traditional society that must be overcome in the
modernization process is the widely shared and often justified
view that outside authority, especially government, is
malevolent.[17] This hostility to authority is typically associated
with a situation of dependency on the same authority. In the
barrios, there is very little of this hostility. The junta is normally
tied to at least one political party, and through that party to some
level of government. The residents believe in cooperation with the
junta. The activities of the police are viewed with favor, and more
police protection is typically desired. Once the barrio is
established—once government makes the critical decision not to
oppose the barrio's formation but instead to give aid such as water
pipes or the loan of a bulldozer for road grading—then the
residents are not only willing to cooperate with authority but even
eager to do so. Development projects for the good of the
"community" that have clear government support are not likely to
founder for want of the residents' interest.

The Claims of the Extended Family. "Familism" is the unpretty
word that stands for concentration on the demands of one's
family to the exclusion of the more outward-looking attitude
required for developmental activity.[18] In the barrio, the extended
family does make important claims. The move to the barrio
often is made with the expectation of assistance from
relatives. Houses are constructed with the aid of the
extended family. But these are manifestations of family
obligations that promote development. The barrios do not, in
fact, show the signs of those family obligations that hinder
the modernization of traditional societies (e. g., the subordi-
nation of individual entrepreneurship to family enterprises or
the duty to share wealth with members of the extended
family). When a man and woman marry, they are expected
to establish their own new household; the nuclear-family-only
living pattern predominates in the barrios, with exceptions
primarily for parents who live with their grown children.

17Rogers, *supra* note 14, at 29-30. See also Kenneth L. Karst and Norris Clement,
"Legal Institutions and Development: Lessons from the Mexican Ejido," *UCLA Law
Review,* 16 (Feb., 1969), 281, 290-293.

18Rogers, *supra* note 14, at 30-31; Lewis, *supra* note 7, at 113-120.

Indeed, a development-minded critic might complain that there is not enough family obligation, as where a man who has casually fathered a child by a woman with whom he is not living feels no sense of duty to support the child, but leaves the child's support to the mother's family. There is some shared sense of obligation to give shelter or even money aid to members of the extended family who are in need, but in the absence of emergency there is no incentive-damping obligation to share income with a wide circle of relatives.[19] If one accumulates wealth, he expects to be able to leave it to his spouse and children upon his death.

The Resident's Perception of Himself

Individual developmental activity is more likely when the individual not only perceives that the situation is not overly threatening, but also perceives himself as someone who is capable of accomplishing his goals. Some of the traits that are desirable from a developmental point of view might be clustered under the heading of "self-confidence." It seems useful, however, to specify these traits with more particularity.

Empathy With Modern Roles. Developmental activity is not to be expected from one who cannot imagine himself in the role of the accumulator of savings, the innovator, the investor. The legal system can promote development by providing institutional support for the maintenance of a self-image that permits him to conceive of engaging in developmental activity. A rigid social stratification not only makes the lower-class individual's advancement objectively more difficult, but also undermines his ability to conceive of something better and therefore his ability to act for the purpose of advancing. Two related ideals, equality and universality, must both appear to represent some significant degree of reality before the lower-class individual will be willing to participate actively in the development process. A legal system thus promotes mobility—and also the *sense* of capacity of men and women at the lower end of the socioeconomic scale—to the degree that it offers opportunities universally. The barrio resident, even the one who has been

[19]Compare Lewis, *supra* note 7, at 113 ff.

a member of the invasion group that founded the barrio on someone else's land, expects that his ownership interests will be protected "just like anyone else's." So he replaces his carton-and-zinc house with concrete blocks; he adds a room; he adds stucco and paint. He cooperates with the junta because everyone is expected to and because he knows that the great majority in fact do cooperate.[20] These institutional supports for individual and collective developmental effort not only produce the immediate benefits sought (a new roof, a new barrio sewer system), but also encourage the attitude that permits the investment in sending children to school. If individual and group effort have a payoff, then education is a road to advancement.

Independence Versus Dependence/Submissiveness. The new resident who is battling the police to keep possession of newly invaded barrio land is anything but submissive. There is an air of independence, in fact, that is discernible merely from walking through a barrio—particularly a barrio that is less than twenty years old. Beyond that age, as the barrio blends into the city, it becomes progressively less a barrio and less distinctive in its atmosphere. The owner of a barrio house "knows his rights" and will stand up for them. The junta's protection of ownership thus reinforces the individual's sense of self-worth; he is as good as anyone else and *entitled* to protection as a right, not a favor to be begged. Correspondingly, when the junta does not offer its legal protection, as in the case of the woman whose husband was mistreating her, the legal system results in encouraging submissiveness. The status of married women in the barrio is not independent; this lack of independence is not peculiar to barrio women, but characterizes married women generally in Venezuela.

Readiness to Take Moderate Risks. Investment implies risk; so does innovation. The requisite development mentality is not that

---

[20]Members of the junta, of course, occupy roles that are quite modern. Nearly one-third of the respondents to the survey stated their willingness (or their spouses' willingness) to become members of the junta. Most of the rest offered excuses (illness, age, too little time). Virtually all the residents understand the essentials of the junta's relations with government and politics. They have a rather sophisticated knowledge of some aspects of national law (the rental of ranchos, the effect of recognition of a child upon inheritance rights).

of the gambler, however—national lotteries are regressive and anti-developmental—but a mentality that perceives the risks of investment and innovation and faces those risks when they are moderate and when the potential return justifies them. The institutional base for developmental risk-taking is a legal system that keeps risks low enough to be sensible. The essence of the barrio housing story is precisely this; the informal legal system provides the tenure security that minimizes the risks of housing investment. The greatest success of the informal legal system, however, may not be in the steady improvement of barrio housing, impressive as that improvement has been. This legal system's greatest success—no less true for its difficulty of being measured—may be in the impact of successful investment upon the attitudes of the hundreds of thousands of barrio investors, who are daily making participatory development a reality. We speak not only of the bodega owner who extends credit to barrio residents or the resident who buys a bicycle on the installment plan, but more fundamentally of the great mass of men and women who are working, accumulating for the future, and investing in their children's education. The Emergency Plan of 1958, by stabilizing expectations concerning land tenure, created not only a favorable climate for housing investment, but significant human resources as well.

Openness to Experience, Alertness to Opportunity. The family that moves to the barrio seizes an opportunity. Furthermore, the successful grasping of one opportunity makes a person more alert to the next one. Everett Hagen associates this kind of openness to experience with the tendency to perceive phenomena as parts of explainable systems—in other words, with the attitude that the world is susceptible to rational manipulation. These are aspects, he says, of creativity.[21] And creativity is one of the obvious characteristics of the entrepreneur, a key figure in economic development.[22] But opportunity exists to be grasped only when there is an institutional structure—an explainable and manipulable system called law—that coerces and rewards in rational ways. The

[21]Hagen, *supra* note 6, at 88.

[22]See generally Joseph A. Schumpeter, *The Theory of Economic Development,* Trans. by Redvers Opie, (Cambridge, Mass.: Harvard University Press, 1934).

81

family that moves to the barrio does so because land appears to be available. And land appears to be available because of a whole series of arrangements that, taken together, permit the judgment that chances are good that the family will be allowed to remain. In the case of an initial invasion, such a calculation by the invaders rests on estimates of the relative clarity of existing claims to title to the land and of the support that can be mustered from certain governmental authorities. In the case of a family that moves to an established barrio, the apparent availability of land rests on a judgment about the present disposition of the barrio as an organized community, usually speaking through the junta.

Willingness to Defer Gratification. Although a family living at the barest subsistence level cannot choose to reduce today's consumption in order to gain an advantage tomorrow, that family does not typify families in the barrios of Caracas. Income levels are high enough to permit some choice, to give the barrio resident the options—denied to the bare-subsistence family—that make him a developmental decision-maker. He may decide not to spend all his income on immediate consumption, but instead to save some of it, or to invest a portion in a concrete floor for his house or in books and school uniforms for his children.[23] The latter decisions require a modern time perspective, one that does not anticipate the future to be merely the endless repetition of the past. Modern institutions of property represent such a shift in time perspective, for they imply stretching the idea of property beyond the thing itself to the capitalized value of its potential future income.[24]

When a barrio resident builds a house and later improves it, he is spending a portion of today's income on tomorrow's enjoyment. He may know perfectly well that he does not have title to the underlying land. Yet there is an institutional base for his investment decision, as we have seen. And his time perspective is modern indeed; he puts money into the materials for his house because he has institutionally secured expectations of quiet enjoyment. An economist

---

[23]The more significant cost of education may be the opportunity cost of foregoing their potential earnings while they are in school. See Theodore W. Schultz, "Investment in Human Capital," *American Economic Review,* 51 (Dec., 1961), 1.

[24]See Commons, *supra* note 5, at 11 ff.

would say that he is assured of the value of the capitalized potential future *imputed* income from the house—the rent he does not have to pay to himself. A lawyer would add only that the assurance takes the form of law.

Even in the barrio, however, there are limits on the residents' willingness to defer to the future. A cooperative work project has the best chance of finding wide support in the barrio when it is simple and perceived to have an early payoff. A project that is very complicated, requiring many months of effort with no possibility for use until the project's completion, would never get beyond the talking stage. Participatory development appears to have this built-in limitation on cooperative work, even though individual families may be willing to scrimp to put their own children through long years of schooling.

The Individual As Member of a Community. For an individual to participate in any cooperative activity, from barrio ditch-digging to voting in a national election, he must feel that he has a personal stake in the outcome of the cooperative enterprise. The barrio residents not only vote, but through their juntas they participate more directly in national political life. The institutional base for this participation includes the junta system itself, plus the organization of government (especially local government) to respond to barrio needs, particularly by allocating funds and materials. Beyond this kind of participation, and more importantly, the barrio people have that kind of stake in the system that comes from a sense of opportunity. National integration is, of course, a developmental goal of great importance, partly independent of the goal of economic growth but also a contributor to that growth. And a sense of opportunity has been called "perhaps the most important single source" of national integration.[25] Among the people of the barrio, as we have shown, the sense of opportunity rests on the expectations secured by law.

[25] Howard Wriggins, "National Integration," in Weiner, *supra* note 8, at 181, 190.

Epilogue

The opening pages of this work referred to two contrasting perceptions of the squatter settlements of Latin America. One school of thought considered them to be urban slums in the process of further decay. Another took a more optimistic position, emphasizing these settlements' positive role in the process of urbanization. Our study of the Caracas barrios falls clearly on the more optimistic side. We have found a set of communities that are, for the most part, characterized by both improvement in living standards and integration with the general urban and national communities.

We began by defining the institutions to be studied in terms that were essentially legal conceptions: property, family obligations, contract, crime, legislation, adjudication. But we have also sought to relate those institutions to their social setting in two ways: studying the rise and decline of an informal barrio legal process; and charting the impact of law on participatory development in the barrios.

When the legal institutions of the barrio are examined from the perspective of changes over time, a rather consistent pattern appears. After the original settlement—whether by invasion, acquiescence, or invitation—a governing junta assumes both legislative and adjudicative functions. Then, within a relatively short period of time, as the barrio merges into the larger metropolis, the residents increasingly look to more traditional governmental authority for support and for the enforcement of their rights.

Moreover, the relationship between law and social development is not a one-way street. In our last chapter, we have emphasized the contributions of the barrio legal process to the participation of barrio residents in two kinds of developmental change: material improvement and integration into the larger community. Thus, while development begets law, law also encourages development. It is the vitality of this process—as we believe to be shown in these pages—that has produced our rather optimistic assessment of barrio life.

84

Appendix A

Methodology

The field work for the study was carried out in 1966-67 and culminated in the summer of 1967. During that summer, three participant-observers lived in three different barrios, and the questionnaire survey was conducted.

Participant Observation. The participant-observers were all UCLA graduate students. Two were law students, and one was an anthropology student; all were fluent in Spanish. Two were former Peace Corps Volunteers, with service in Ecuador, the Dominican Republic and Panama; the third was a native Chilean. Each involved himself to the maximum possible extent in the life of his barrio, helping with community projects such as road building, a barrio census, or even the planning of a fiesta.

The participant-observers focused on the same general subject areas as those covered by the survey questionnaire, so that their observations were cross-checks on the results of the survey. (One of these three barrios was included in the survey.) Furthermore, the participant-observers were able to probe delicately into some topics that were too sensitive for a structured questionnaire interview. They also followed particular events and transactions, making a special effort to become acquainted with the operations of the various barrio juntas in order to provide an inside view of that institution to complement the picture produced by the survey of the barrio residents' attitudes toward the junta.

The Survey. The first draft of the questionnaire was written a full year before the survey was to be taken. Although in English, it was written jointly by Venezuelans and North Americans. All six succeeding drafts were written in Spanish. The final draft—following a pre-test of the penultimate draft in a pilot barrio—was written with the aid of Venezuelan sociologists. This final questionnaire consisted mainly of highly structured rather than open-ended items. The following areas were covered:

1. Personal data about the interviewee and his (her) family. Migration history; age, sex, education, and employment of each member of the household.

2. History of affording housing to relatives or others; willingness to do so in the future. Expectations that relatives or others would house the interviewee in case of need; history of such a case. Persons contributing to the maintenance of the house.
3. Occupancy of land and house. Who owns the land, the house? How was the land obtained? Title disputes, if any; sense of security about future occupancy. Rental arrangements. Past or expected investment in housing (added room, improved roof, etc.). Expectations about devolution of property upon death.
4. Commercial relations, emphasizing short-term credit and remedies in case of a merchant's cheating.
5. Theft in the barrio. Past experience, past and expected remedies.
6. Cash borrowing. Terms of repayment, interest, creditors' remedies.
7. Physical security. Involvement of members of the family in fights; obligation to aid a relative in a fight. Sense of security within the barrio. Relations with the police.
8. Marriage obligations of husband and wife; effect of legal marriage on obligations; informal sanctions against infidelity. Pregnancy of an unmarried daughter: parents' sanctions, legal or otherwise; attitudes toward abortion, contraception.
9. The barrio junta. Activities, residents' evaluations of the junta's work. Attitudes toward cooperation.
10. General matters: Income of the household; type of housing construction; location of house within the barrio.

The questionnaire was administered to 622 interviewees in ten barrios which had been selected purposively, not randomly, according to a range of characteristics bearing some postulated significant relation to the barrios' internal legal system. An initial typology of the barrios of Caracas based on six potential variables was ultimately reduced to a typology based on three factors: population size, quality of public service, and proximity to centers of employment and shopping.[1]

---

[1]This typology was later carried over into a general typology of the Caracas barrios. See Henry Sarmiento, "Tipología de los Barrios de Caracas," in *Boletín*, (Caracas: Centro Latinoamericano de Venezuela—CLAVE, 1969). Compare Rosa Elena Hidalgo and Alberto Gruson, *Barrios Populares de Caracas: Módulos Sociales de Operación*, (Caracas: Centro de Informaciones en Ciencias Sociales—CISOR, 1969).

Each of these three factors was assigned a value from one to three. A very large barrio that had good public services and was quite close to the urban centers was assigned a code of 111; a small barrio with poor public services and located on the city's fringes had a code of 333. The possible combinations in this scheme, of course, total twenty-seven. In fact, on the basis of a sample of some 200 barrios, some twenty-four types were found; of these, only sixteen types were represented by more than two barrios in the sample. The selection of ten barrios was aimed at producing a variety of types within this framework. It was also decided to try to make some minimal use of other factors, including some that had been initially discarded; that is, seeking to include some barrios with strong community organization and others with little or none, and also seeking some diversity in barrio terrain and in the age of the barrios surveyed.

Within each barrio to be surveyed, the interviewees were chosen on a systematic basis. In the largest barrio (some 2000 houses), the sample was 7.5 percent of all households in the barrio, for a total of 150 interviews. In the smallest barrios, the sample surveyed was more than 30 percent of the households. The overall sample in all ten barrios came out to be about 15 percent. A 20 percent sample, for example, was secured by going to every fifth house on every street or pathway and counting two-family buildings as two households. A 28 percent sample was obtained by going to every third house, then every fourth house, then every third house, etc. The interviewers were acquainted with the dangers of biasing the sample, such as by omitting a particular house because it looked like a disagreeable place for an interview or for some other reason. The instructions to the interviewers at the orientation session gave great emphasis to the need for maintaining the purity of the systematic nature of the sample. If a resident was away from the house, the interviewer returned later in the same day to secure the interview; barrio residents rarely leave their houses unattended for long periods, and this method was normally successful in preserving the sample.

Two teams of interviewers, all twenty-three of whom were sociology students at the Andrés Bello Catholic University in Caracas, were used. All were experienced in survey-taking, and about half had worked previously on surveys in barrios. Fourteen were women and nine were men.

Each barrio was surveyed in a single day, and the entire survey was completed in five days. In substantial part, the dispatch with which the interviews were conducted was due to the cooperation of the barrio residents; the rejection rate was under 4 percent. Women comprised 59 percent of the interviewees, and men, 41 percent. The median age of the interviewees was thirty-six, and the median age of the heads of household was thirty-eight.

The questionnaires were coded in Caracas and the data keypunched in Los Angeles. Statistical analyses were carried out at the Campus Computing Network, University of California, Los Angeles.

The text of the questionnaire appears in Appendix B, along with the distribution of responses for the total sample. Appendix C contains selected questionnaire items with the distribution of responses cross-classified by the age of the barrio.

Appendix B

Questionnaire with Distribution of Responses

	N	%
1.01. Region where interviewee spent most of his or her years between ages 5 and 15:		
Metropolitan District (D.F. and Sucre District of State of Miranda)	154	27.7
Central (Miranda, Aragua, Carabobo, Yaracuy)	144	25.9
West (Zulia, Lara, Falcón)	47	8.5
Plains (Guárico, Cojedes, Apure, Portuguesa, Barinas)	22	4.0
Andes (Mérida, Táchira, Trujillo)	108	19.5
East (Sucre, Nueva Esparta, Anzoátegui, Monagas)	58	10.5
Guayana (Bolívar, Amazonas, Delta Amacuro)	8	1.4
Another country	14	2.5
Size and characteristics of the place where he or she spent most of the years between ages 5 and 15:		
Caracas (in a barrio)	89	16.3
Caracas (other than in a barrio)	61	11.2
Other city (over 20,000 population in 1960)	99	18.1
Pueblo (so identified if it has a plaza)	255	46.7
Village or countryside	42	7.7
Total time in Caracas (not in barrios):		
up to one year	118	36.0
1-3 years	43	13.1
4-6 years	52	15.9
7-9 years	23	7.0
10-12 years	20	6.1
13-15 years	18	5.5
16-18 years	10	3.0
19-21 years	12	3.7
22 years or more	32	9.8
Total time in Caracas (in barrios):		
up to one year	24	4.7
1-3 years	45	8.8
4-6 years	73	14.2

	N	%
7-9 years	75	14.6
10-12 years	57	11.1
13-15 years	49	9.5
16-18 years	31	6.0
19-21 years	36	7.0
22 years or more	124	24.1

1.02. How long have you been in this barrio?

	N	%
up to 3 months	38	6.2
3-6 months	33	5.4
6 months-1 year	34	5.5
1-3 years	119	19.4
4-6 years	138	22.5
7-9 years	62	10.1
10-12 years	53	8.6
13-15 years	29	4.7
16 years or more	108	17.6

1.03. How long have you lived in this house?

	N	%
up to 3 months	47	7.6
3-6 months	47	7.6
6 months-1 year	53	8.6
1-3 years	137	22.3
4-6 years	135	22.0
7-9 years	59	9.6
10-12 years	37	6.0
13-15 years	24	3.9
16 years or more	76	12.4

1.04. Why did you move to *this* barrio?

	N	%
Matrimonial reasons ("I got married"; *not*, "I came with my husband so he could find work")	46	7.7
Family (non-matrimonial) reasons	98	16.4
Friends in the barrio	6	1.0
Land (or house) available here (not "We bought here," but "We looked, and found land here" — or an economic reason for buying here, such as the cost of housing)	191	31.9
Location near work, situation in the city, proximity of transportation (a determined job — not just that there was no work in the old place)	36	6.0
Conditions of the barrio (school, other services, physical security, climate, people, "atmosphere")	53	8.8

	N	%
The government put us here	2	.3
Other	100	16.7
Inadequate answer	167	27.9

1.05. Did you come here alone or with your family?

Alone	82	13.6
With family	520	86.4

1.06. Number of persons living in the house:

1	13	2.1
2	31	5.0
3	48	7.7
4	70	11.3
5	76	12.3
6	85	13.7
7	64	10.3
8	69	11.1
9	49	7.9
10	32	5.2
11 or more	83	13.2

Sex of interviewee:

Male	253	40.8
Female	367	59.2

Sex of head of the family:

Male	495	80.4
Female	120	19.5

Age of interviewee:

14-19	13	.2
20-29	177	28.6
30-39	197	32.1
40-49	130	21.0
50-59	59	9.5
60-69	32	5.2
70-86	10	1.8

Age of head of the family:

19-29	137	22.5
30-39	203	33.1
40-49	155	25.3
50-59	66	10.8
60-69	43	7.2
70-86	9	1.6

	N	%
Civil status of the head of the family (as stated by the interviewee):		
Bachelor (living in *concubinato*)	199	32.3
Bachelor (not living in *concubinato* in this house)	101	16.4
Married	243	39.4
Unido or *unida* (common-law marriage)	40	6.5
Divorced	6	1.0
Widow(er)	25	4.1
Other (e.g., married to another man, but separated)	2	.3
Civil status of the interviewee (as stated by the interviewee):		
Bachelor (living in *concubinato*)	192	31.2
Bachelor (not living in *concubinato*)	109	17.7
Married	239	38.8
Unido or *unida*	39	6.3
Divorced	9	1.5
Widow(er)	26	4.2
Other	2	.3
Relation of the interviewee to head of family:		
The head of the family himself (herself)	342	55.5
Wife or husband	248	40.3
Son or daughter	13	2.1
Other relative	12	1.9
No relation	1	.2
Persons living in the house (mark the lowest on the list that is applicable):		
Only the nuclear family (husband, wife, children)	286	46.2
Nuclear family (n.f.) plus other paying relatives	49	7.9
N.f. plus non-paying relatives	109	17.6
N.f. plus paying *compadres* (including *ahijados* and *padrinos*)	4	.6
N.f. plus other persons who pay	3	.5
N.f. plus other persons who do not pay	29	4.7
Other (includes father with children, no mother)	51	8.2
Mother with children, no father	40	6.5
Mother with children, no father, plus other persons, relatives or not, paying or not	48	7.8
Education of head of the family:		
Illiterate	11	3.0
Can read and write, and/or 1 year primary	17	4.6

	N	%
2d or 3d grade, primary	65	17.5
4th, 5th or 6th grade, primary	168	45.3
Bachillerato (incomplete)	76	20.5
Bachillerato (completed)	7	1.9
University (any year) and/or technical school	4	1.1
Special studies that do not require completion of primary grades	3	.8
Special studies that do require primary (completed)	20	5.4

Education of the child with the most years of instruction:

	N	%
Illiterate	11	3.0
Can read or write, and/or 1 year primary	17	4.6
2d or 3d grade, primary	65	17.5
4th, 5th or 6th grade, primary	168	45.3
Bachillerato (incomplete)	76	20.5
Bachillerato (completed)	7	1.9
University (any year) and/or technical school	4	1.1
Special studies that do not require completion of primary grades	3	.8
Special studies that do require primary (completed)	20	5.4

Children's surnames:

	N	%
All children have the surname of the mother	141	26.9
All children have the surname of the present spouse of the mother (husband or *unido*)	311	59.2
Some of the children have the surname of the present husband, etc., and others have the mother's surname	50	9.5
Other	23	4.4

Occupation of the head of the family:

	N	%
Unskilled worker	157	26.5
Skilled worker	82	13.9
Comerciante (has own business)	24	4.1
Chauffeur, or unskilled white-collar employee (bill collector, shop salesman, messenger, office boy)	148	25.0
Skilled white-collar employee (secretary, cashier)	18	3.0
Street vendor	22	3.7
Professional (teacher, nurse)	11	1.9
Domestic	33	5.6
Sub-employment (ironing, making *arepas*, etc.)	8	1.4
Housewife	54	9.1

	N	%
Don't know (or no answer)	5	.8
Public employment (e.g., policeman)	24	4.1
Other (includes student)	6	1.0

Is the head of the family employed at the moment?

	N	%
No	172	27.9
Yes	444	72.1

Number of persons living in the house who are employed at the moment:

	N	%
0	65	10.5
1	308	49.9
2	138	22.4
3	63	10.2
4	28	4.5
5	10	1.6
6	4	.6
7	1	.2

1.07. Do you intend to move from this barrio during the coming year?

	N	%
Yes	215	35.1
No	296	48.3
Conditional yes ("if we sell")	13	2.1
Other	2	.3
Don't know (includes "perhaps")	87	14.2

(If yes) Why?

	N	%
Present house is inadequate, or rent is too high	50	26.2
Physical environment is bad in this barrio (steep hill, dirty, etc.)	34	17.8
Lack of services (water, light, toilets, etc.)	5	2.6
Lack of a school	4	2.1
Moral environment, danger, etc. (includes "very dangerous here," and "bad environment for children")	43	22.5
Distance from work, or from transport	7	3.7
The government may eject us	3	1.6
Wants to have own house	14	7.3
Other	31	16.2

				N	%

2.01. Apart from the people living in your house now, have you ever given lodging here in the house to anyone else for more than a month? (If yes, to whom?)

No — 342 | 57.9

	Responses					
	1st		2d		3d	
	N	%	N	%	N	%
(If yes)						
Relatives	141	56.6	20	30.3	5	27.8
In-laws, relatives by marriage	28	11.2	19	28.8	2	11.1
Compadres	7	2.8	8	12.1	1	5.5
Friends, acquaintances	54	21.7	13	19.7	8	44.4
Neighbors (same barrio)	4	1.6	1	1.5	1	5.5
Persons from the same state	10	4.0	3	4.5	1	5.5
Anyone who needed it	3	1.2	2	3.0	–	–
Other	2	.8	–	–	–	–

(If yes) And did they pay anything?

Yes — 37 | 17.2
No — 177 | 82.3

2.02. And would you be disposed to give lodging here in the house to anyone, in any case, for more than a month, without their having to pay you? (If yes, to whom?)

No — 260 | 49.5

	Responses					
	1st		2d		3d	
	N	%	N	%	N	%
(If yes)						
Relatives	173	78.3	24	22.8	5	18.5
In-laws, relatives by marriage	18	8.1	42	40.0	3	11.1
Compadres	1	.4	3	2.8	2	7.4
Friends, acquaintances	26	11.8	27	25.7	11	40.7
Neighbors (same barrio)	2	.9	5	4.8	1	3.7
Persons from the same state	1	.4	4	3.8	5	18.5

	1st		2d		3d		N	%
	N	%	N	%	N	%		
Anyone who needed it	31	70.4	18	90.0	3	100.0		
Other	13	29.5	2	10.0	–	–		

2.03 Has anyone ever helped you by giving you lodging in their house for more than a month? (If yes, who?)

No ... 426 | 70.9

Responses

	1st		2d		3d	
	N	%	N	%	N	%
(If yes)						
Relatives	85	48.6	5	22.7	4	50.0
Relatives by marriage	28	16.0	7	31.8	1	12.5
Compadres	12	6.8	4	18.2	1	12.5
Friends, acquaintances	42	24.0	2	9.1	1	12.5
Neighbors (same barrio)	3	1.7	1	4.5	–	–
Persons from same state	2	1.1	2	9.1	–	–
Other	3	1.7	1	4.5	1	12.5

2.04 And would anyone be willing to lodge you in their house for a long time, in case of need? (If yes, who?)

No ... 259 | 52.7

Responses

	1st		2d		3d	
	N	%	N	%	N	%
(If yes)						
Relatives	168	72.0	13	27.7	2	28.5
In-laws, relatives by marriage	16	6.9	13	27.7	1	14.3
Compadres	8	3.4	3	6.4	2	28.5
Friends, acquaintances	21	9.0	13	27.7	1	14.3
Neighbors (same barrio)	5	2.2	3	6.4	1	14.3
Persons from same state	1	.4	2	4.2	–	–
Other	13	5.6	–	–	–	–

	N	%

2.05. Apart from the persons who live in this house, is there anyone else who gives money to maintain the house?

	N	%
No	515	86.6
(If yes, mark first name given)		
Father of one or more children of the woman who lives in the house	26	4.4
Relative of the interviewee's side of the family	18	3.0
Relative of the spouse's side of the family	5	.8
Child	16	2.7
Mother or father of a grandchild	1	.2
In-law	3	.5
Compadre (includes *ahijados*, etc.)	3	.5
Other	8	1.3

2.06. In case of great economic necessity (sickness, etc.), and if no one in your family could help you, to whom would you go? (First response.)

	N	%
No one	113	23.0
Neighbor (same barrio)	72	14.7
Fellow worker	54	11.0
Politician	3	.6
The junta	8	1.6
The government (undifferentiated)	52	10.6
A named government agency	50	10.2
Other	89	18.1
Don't know	50	10.2

3.01. Who is the owner of this land?

	N	%
No one	11	1.8
I	74	12.2
Spouse of interviewee	23	3.8
Relative	34	5.6
Other named person	112	18.5
The municipality	75	12.4
The government (not municipal)	10	1.7
Land title is in litigation, or owner is unknown	9	1.5
Don't know	257	42.5

3.02. Whose house is this?

	N	%
Mine	384	62.7
Spouse of interviewee	50	8.2
Relative	60	9.8
Other person living in the barrio	52	8.5

	N	%
Other person living outside barrio	57	9.3
Other	9	1.4

Is the same person stated to be the owner of both the land and the house?

	N	%
No	410	67.3
Yes	172	28.2
Unknown	27	4.4

3.03. How did you acquire this land?

	N	%
I (we) bought the house	212	36.0
I (we) bought the land	40	6.8
I (we) paid for the leveling of the land	29	4.9
The house is rented	83	14.1
The land was a relative's, and he gave it to us	21	3.6
The junta assigned us to it	31	5.3
A government authority assigned us to it	23	3.9
We occupied the land	104	17.7
Other	46	7.8

(If "We occupied") How — alone, or in a group?

	N	%
Alone	71	55.5
In a group	57	44.5

(If "We occupied") And did you have any problems with the authorities or with the junta?

	N	%
No	74	64.3
Yes	41	35.7

3.05. Has the owner of the land ever come and asked you to pay him?

	N	%
No	343	84.5
Yes	47	11.6
Don't know	16	3.9

3.06. If the owner of the land came and asked you to pay him, what would you do?

	N	%
We would move	55	18.0
The owner would have to pay us the value of the house	9	3.0
We would pay for the land (without conditions), or, we would pay if everyone else did	148	48.5
We would pay for the land if he could prove he was the owner	18	5.9
We would pay for the land if he would set a fair price (or give time to pay, etc.)	24	7.9

	N	%

	N	%
We would do whatever the junta said to do	3	1.0
We would reach an agreement (without specifying sale of the house or purchase of the land)	8	2.6
We would go to the authorities (police, etc.)	10	3.3
Don't know	30	9.8

3.07. Have you ever had an argument with anyone over your right to build on this land or to live in this house? (If yes: To whom did you go to resolve the problem?)

	N	%
No	561	90.4
(If yes)		
The junta	13	2.1
The police (a policeman)	5	.8
A court	7	1.1
The *jefatura*, municipal council	14	2.3
Another government authority	2	.3
A neighbor (same barrio)	4	.6
Other	14	2.3

(If no) If you had an argument of this type, to whom would you go?

	N	%
The junta	63	14.0
The police	35	7.8
A court	14	3.1
The municipal council	119	26.5
Another government authority	48	10.7
A neighbor (same barrio)	9	2.0
Don't know	161	35.8

3.08. (If house not owned by interviewee)

Do you pay something in rent?

	N	%
No	32	23.9
Yes	101	75.4
Don't know	1	.7

3.09. (If yes) Do you have a written contract with the owner specifying the rent?

	N	%
No	93	76.9
Yes	27	22.3
Don't know	1	.8

	N	%

(If no) But is there some other condition, besides the payment of rent, that you have to fulfill?

	N	%
No	79	79.8
Yes	18	18.2
Don't know	2	2.0

3.10. Does the owner of this house live in the barrio?

	N	%
No	70	56.9
Yes	51	41.5
Other	2	1.6

3.11. Although you were to pay rent, could the owner make you get out for the following reasons?

(a) Damage to property

	N	%
No	49	52.7
Yes	35	37.6
Don't know	6	6.5
Other	3	3.2

(b) Unforeseen use of the property?

	N	%
No	50	57.5
Yes	32	36.8
Don't know	5	5.7
Other	—	—

3.12. If you were unable to pay the rent, would you have to move?

	N	%
No	27	25.2
Yes	75	70.1
Don't know	3	2.8
Other	2	1.9

3.13. In any of the barrios where you have rented a house, has the owner ever tried to raise the rent? (If yes, what happened?)

	N	%
No	97	82.9
(If yes)		
I paid	10	8.5
I refused to pay	2	1.7
I came to an agreement with the landlord	1	.9
I resorted to the junta	—	—
I resorted to another authority	2	1.7
I moved	4	3.4
Other	1	.9

100

		N	%

3.14. And what would you do if the owner tried to raise
the rent?

	N	%
I would pay	22	21.2
I wouldn't pay (without specification)	4	3.8
I would try to settle the matter, or arrive at a fair price, etc.	15	14.4
I would resort to the junta	1	1.0
I would resort to another authority	6	5.8
I would move	45	43.3
Other	11	10.6

3.15. Have any big improvements or additions been made
in this house?

	N	%
No	91	74.0
Yes	32	26.0

3.16. (If yes) How did you get the materials?

	N	%
We bought them	23	65.7
The owner brought them	9	25.7
They were given to me	3	8.6
Other	—	—

3.18. (If tenant paid for materials) Did you ask the
owner to pay for the materials or the work?

	N	%
No	21	72.4
Yes	7	24.1
Don't know	—	—
Other	1	3.4

3.20. (If interviewee owns the house) Did you buy or
build this house? (If he or she built it) Who
worked on the construction?

	N	%
Bought it	157	32.4
(If built)		
Interviewee built it alone, or with his (her) nuclear family only	109	22.5
Built it with paid labor (even if a relative)	122	25.2
Built it with help of unpaid relatives	66	13.6
Built it with help of unpaid *compadre(s)*	5	1.0
Built it with help of unpaid neighbor(s)	2	.4
Built it with help of other unpaid persons	15	3.1
Other	8	1.7

	N	%

3.22. Have you added any important additions to the house? ("Important" means ceiling, cement blocks, cement floor, another room) If so, what?

	N	%
No	136	28.4
One important improvement	172	35.9
Two important improvements	92	19.2
Three or more important improvements	79	16.5

3.23. Do you intend to add any important additions to the house?

	N	%
No	130	27.5
Yes	336	71.2
Don't know	4	.8
Other	2	.4

3.24. If in some case a road (or something like that) were to be put through here by the government, would you expect the government to pay you something for the land? (If yes) How would you arrive at a price?

	N	%
No	283	59.5
Don't know	15	3.2
(If yes)		
The government would set the price	31	6.5
I (we) would set the price	24	5.0
They would pay me what it cost me	13	2.7
We would have to come to an agreement	44	9.2
Yes, but don't know how the price would be set	51	10.7
Other	15	3.2

3.25. And would you expect to be paid something for the house? (If yes) How would the price be fixed?

	N	%
No	8	1.7
Don't know if government would pay	18	3.7
(If yes)		
The government would decide on the price	99	20.5
I (we) would decide	37	7.6
They would pay me what I have spent on the house	229	47.3
We would come to an agreement	14	2.9
Don't know how the price would be set	66	13.6
Other	13	2.7

		N	%
3.26.	And if the government paid you something, what would you do with the money?		
	Construction or purchase of a new house	466	95.3
	Other	17	3.5
	Don't know	6	1.2
3.27.	If you died, to whom would you leave your belongings (the house) as inheritance?		
	Children	422	70.5
	Spouse	55	9.2
	Children and spouse	51	8.5
	Other relative	59	9.8
	Other person	2	.3
	Other answer	5	.8
	Don't know	5	.8
3.28.	(If interviewee doesn't answer children or spouse) Why?		
	Children are minors	20	24.7
	I am grateful to them	9	11.1
	They are my nearest relatives	38	46.9
	Other	14	17.3
3.29.	Have you done anything to see that your goods will pass to those persons? (If yes) What?		
	No	532	90.8
	(If yes)		
	The children are legitimate (recognized)	13	2.2
	Life insurance, or bank account	9	1.5
	Will	13	2.2
	I've talked with relatives (friends), and they will take care of the children	2	.3
	Other	17	2.9
	(If no) Are you thinking of doing anything? (If yes) What?		
	No, without specifying why	218	40.1
	No, let the children divide everything among themselves	9	1.7
	No, because the children are legitimate	7	1.3
	(If yes)		
	Life insurance or bank account	3	.6
	Will	30	5.5
	Sign some paper or document	182	33.5

	N	%

Talk to relatives or friends to make sure children are cared for	4	.7
Other	51	9.4
Don't know	39	7.2

4.01. Where do you buy food?

Within the barrio	213	34.9
Outside the barrio	354	58.0
Both within and outside the barrio	40	6.6
Other	3	.5

(If outside the barrio) Where?

Bodega	76	17.5
Mercado libre	287	66.0
Both *bodega* and *mercado libre*	36	8.3
Other	36	8.3

4.02. Do you always pay cash for food or does the storekeeper give you credit?

Always buy for cash	447	73.0
Sometimes the *bodeguero* gives credit	120	19.6
Regularly the *bodeguero* gives credit	40	6.5
Other	5	.8

4.03. If you had no money, would the storekeeper be inclined to give you credit?

No	164	34.5
Yes	263	55.4
Don't know	43	9.1
Other	5	1.1

4.04. And if you were given credit, and you could not pay, what would happen?

Nothing	36	12.3
They would take the things back	17	5.8
They would wait for their money	117	39.9
They would have me jailed	12	4.1
They wouldn't give me more credit	42	14.3
Don't know	10	3.4
Other	59	20.1

4.05. When you buy things that are very expensive (radio, TV, furniture, etc.), do you pay cash or by installments?

Cash	131	22.5
Installments	451	77.5

	N	%

4.06. What happens if a person cannot continue paying
the installments?

	N	%
Nothing	23	4.1
They take away the thing	480	86.2
Don't know	20	3.6
They put him in jail	3	.5
Other	31	5.6

4.07. Have you ever bought something and then thought
that they had tricked you as to the price or the
quantity of what they gave you? (that they had
cheated you?)

	N	%
No	475	80.9
Yes	112	19.1

(If yes) What was your reaction?

	N	%
Nothing	64	53.3
I complained to the one who sold it to me	32	26.7
I complained to the police	5	4.2
I complained to another authority	10	8.3
Other	9	7.5

4.08. If you had arguments about these things (being
cheated, arguments about credit), to whom would
you go to solve the problem? (First response)

	N	%
No one	87	19.0
A neighbor (same barrio)	13	2.8
A relative	19	4.1
The police (a policeman)	136	29.6
The junta	6	1.3
The *jefatura*, or municipal council	49	10.7
The market authorities	18	3.9
The courts	29	6.3
Complain to the seller	102	22.2

5.01.– Have you ever had something stolen? (If yes)
5.03. Did you have an idea who took it? (If yes)
Did the person live in the barrio? Was it an
acquaintance? A relative?

	N	%
Has had nothing stolen	445	74.7
Yes, but has no idea who took it	90	15.1
Yes, and it was an acquaintance	44	7.4
Yes, and it was a friend	14	2.3
Yes, and it was a relative	3	.5

	N	%

5.04. (If yes to first question in 5.01) What did you do?

	N	%
Nothing	103	64.8
I went to look for it myself	12	7.5
I went to the police (a policeman)	39	24.5
I went to the junta	2	1.3
I went to court	1	.6
I went to the government (agency unspecified)	2	1.3

5.05. And what happened?

	N	%
The thing was not recovered	106	86.2
I got it back	10	8.1
Other	7	5.7

5.06. And if something were to be stolen, what would you do?

	N	%
Nothing (resignation)	106	24.7
Nothing, since no one would help	23	5.4
Look for it myself	19	4.4
Go to the police	236	55.0
Go to court	2	.5
Go to the government (no agency specified)	17	4.0
It depends on the value of the thing; if it is valuable, I'd go to the police	16	3.7
Other	10	2.3

6.01. Have you ever sought to borrow money in an amount of more than Bs. 1000? (If yes) What did you use it for? (Use most recent example)

	N	%
No	364	60.4
(If yes)		
To build (buy) a house	85	14.1
To pay for sickness, or funeral	36	6.0
To use in business	11	1.8
For food, clothing	28	4.6
For other consumer's goods	52	8.6
To send money to my family	4	.7
Other	23	3.8

6.02. (If yes) And did you have to give anything as guarantee?

	N	%
No	194	82.6
Yes	38	16.2
Other	3	1.3

	N	%

6.03. From whom did you get the loan?

	N	%
Private lender (or employer)	26	11.1
Bank	6	2.6
Friend (or co-worker)	58	24.8
Relative	30	12.8
Compadre	15	6.4
Savings bank	91	38.9
Bodeguero or other seller	3	1.3
The C.V.F. (a government agency)	1	.4
Other	4	1.7

6.04– And were you able to return it? (If yes) How, in
6.05   cash or in installments?

	N	%
No	11	4.6
(If yes)		
In cash	74	31.2
In installments	149	62.9
Other	3	1.3

6.06. Did you have to return the money within a
specified time?

	N	%
No	111	51.2
Yes	106	48.8
Other	–	–

(If yes) How much time did they give you to pay?

	N	%
Some weeks (up to a month)	26	23.0
A month to one year	68	60.2
More than a year	8	7.1
According to my ability to pay	7	6.2
Other	4	3.5

6.08. Did you have to repay more than was lent to you?

	N	%
No	166	76.5
Yes	51	23.5
Don't know	–	–

7.01. Has anyone in the family (living in the house) ever
been involved in a serious fight (that came to blows)?
(If yes) Who fought?

	N	%
No	524	89.7
(If yes)		
Man, husband	34	5.8
Woman, wife	7	1.2
Son, son-in-law	10	1.7

	N	%

Daughter, daughter-in-law — | —
Other — | —

7.02. With whom was the fight?

	N	%
Relative	10	17.9
Friend	7	12.5
Neighbor (same barrio)	26	46.4
Acquaintance	4	7.1
Various persons	1	1.8
Other	8	14.3

7.03. Why did they fight?

	N	%
Self-defense	15	25.9
Family quarrel	2	3.4
Over a woman	4	6.9
Influence of alcohol	19	32.8
Aiding other persons	6	10.3
Over ownership of property	2	3.4
Other	10	17.2

7.04. And when someone in the family has been involved in a serious fight, did anyone help him (her)? (If yes) Who?

	N	%
No	30	46.2
(If yes)		
Relatives	19	29.2
Compadres	1	1.5
Friends	9	13.8
Neighbors (same barrio)	3	4.6
Unknown person	—	—
Some authority (police, junta)	2	3.1
Other	1	1.5

7.06. What could be done to make the barrio more safe?

	N	%
More police vigilance	263	64.8
Change the junta	1	.2
Change the government	3	.7
Put in a school	5	1.2
Let each one dedicate himself to his own work (or not interfere with others)	38	9.4
Let parents educate their children	10	2.5
Don't know	44	10.8
Nothing	25	6.2

	N	%

7.09. What is your opinion about the way in which the police have acted in the barrio?

	N	%
There are no police here	47	8.2
Very good	49	8.6
Good	212	37.1
All right (*regular*)	148	25.9
Bad	65	11.4
Very bad	28	4.9
Don't know	17	3.0
Says "good" but also complains of police failures	5	.9

7.10. Is there another person (other than police) to whom people go in order to resolve a problem or an argument that might lead to a serious fight? (If yes) To whom?

	N	%
No	289	48.9
(If yes)		
The junta	145	24.5
The government (an agency)	6	1.0
The *jefatura* or municipal council	64	10.8
A neighbor (same barrio)	46	7.8
Depends on the problem	1	.2
Other	40	6.8

7.11. And do the police put people in jail without reason?

	N	%
Always (regularly)	47	8.9
Sometimes	126	23.7
Occasionally (*pocas veces*)	26	4.9
Never	303	57.1
Other	29	5.5

And when there is a problem, do the police help resolve it?

	N	%
Always (regularly)	171	34.6
Sometimes	141	28.5
Occasionally	51	10.3
Never	104	21.1
Other	27	5.5

8.01. Suppose a man and a woman live together (are
       unidos). How do you think the man should behave?
       That is, what obligations does the man have to
       fulfill?

	Responses					
	1st		2d		3d	
	N	%	N	%	N	%
Inadequate answer (e.g., fulfill the duties of the home)	123	20.4	35	7.0	17	6.8
Bring home money (food, clothes)	278	46.0	158	31.7	30	12.0
Behave well (be serious, stay home, don't get drunk)	107	17.7	61	12.2	33	13.3
Fidelity	4	.7	5	1.0	2	.8
Respect the woman	19	3.1	27	5.4	19	7.6
Love and affection, avoid arguments, be nice, don't hit the woman	18	3.0	43	8.6	20	8.0
Marry the woman	25	4.1	3	.6	5	2.0
Educate the children	9	1.5	61	12.2	44	17.7
Take care of the children, be affectionate to them, discipline them	21	3.5	105	21.1	79	31.7

8.02. And how should the woman behave, that is, what
       do you think are her obligations?

	Responses					
	1st		2d		3d	
	N	%	N	%	N	%
Same obligations as the man	45	8.7	6	2.1	1	1.2
Take care of the home, make meals, wash, iron, market, etc.	238	46.2	122	43.6	29	35.0
Look after the husband, be considerate	177	34.4	106	37.8	27	33.8
Respect the husband, obey him, avoid arguments	55	10.7	46	16.4	24	30.0

		Responses					N	%
	1st		2d		3d			
	N	%	N	%	N	%		
Stay home	17	17.7	24	13.1	13	10.9		
Fidelity	13	13.5	6	3.3	8	6.7		
Take care of the children (or, her children)	41	42.7	129	70.5	86	72.3		
Work outside the home if she can	5	5.2	5	2.7	4	3.4		
Other	20	20.8	19	10.4	8	6.7		

8.03. And if they get married by law, do you think that then the man would have new obligations to fulfill? (If yes) Which?

	N	%
No	385	68.0
(If yes)		
Without specifying	64	11.3
Same obligations, but with greater responsibility	56	9.9
The house then belongs to both	2	.4
Give money to the wife	6	1.1
More respect to the home, or to the wife	25	4.4
Remain with the wife; fidelity	21	3.7
Take care of the children	3	.5
Don't know	4	.7

8.04. And would the woman have new obligations when she is married by law, or not? (If yes) Which?

	N	%
No	433	72.2
(If yes)		
Without specifying	46	7.7
Same obligations as before, but with greater responsibility	30	5.0
The same new obligations as the man	8	1.3
More respect for the husband, behave well	44	7.3
Fidelity	12	2.0
More attention to the children	5	.8
More *rights* (not asked for, but volunteered by some)	17	2.8
Don't know	5	.8

		N	%

8.05. Suppose a man lives in a house with a woman, and that he brings a second woman to live in the same house. What do you think would happen?

	N	%
The first woman would accept the situation	12	2.1
Some would accept it, others not	7	1.2
The first would throw the second out	168	29.2
One of the two would have to leave	31	5.4
Expressions of disgust, but without answering the question explicitly (e.g., they would fight)	165	28.7
The first woman would throw out the man (or both the man and the second woman)	66	11.5
Resort to the authorities (or the law)	24	4.2
The first would leave	89	15.5
Don't know	13	2.3

8.06. What would the neighbors do? Do you think they would continue visiting the house?

	N	%
No	370	62.5
Yes	153	25.8
Some yes, some no	7	1.2
Sometimes yes, sometimes no (or, "it depends")	24	4.1
Other	5	.8
Don't know	33	5.6

Would the neighbors continue to have anything to do with the man in this case?

	N	%
No	302	52.2
Yes	182	31.3
Some yes, some no	8	1.4
Sometimes yes, sometimes no (or, "it depends")	34	5.9
Other	18	3.1
Don't know	36	6.2

8.07. And if the man brought the second woman to live in the same barrio, or lived with another woman in the same barrio, what do you think would happen?

	N	%
The first woman would accept the situation	112	21.3
Some would accept it, others not	13	2.5
The man would have to choose one	7	1.3
Expressions of disgust, without answering explicitly	137	26.0
The first woman would abandon the man (or throw him out)	148	28.1
Resort to the authorities	6	1.1

	N	%

	N	%
If they were married, the first would divorce the man	6	1.1
The first would try to make the second woman leave the barrio	73	13.9
Don't know	24	4.6

8.08. And would the neighbors continue seeing the man in this case?

	N	%
No	224	38.6
Yes	265	45.6
Some yes, others no	10	1.7
Sometimes yes, sometimes no	33	5.7
Other	6	1.0
Don't know	43	7.4

8.09. And what would happen if he had another woman in another barrio?

	N	%
The first woman would accept the situation	209	40.5
Some would accept it, others not	14	2.7
The man would have to choose one	6	1.2
Expressions of disgust, unspecified	56	10.9
The first woman would abandon the man (or throw him out)	66	12.8
Resort to the authorities	5	1.0
If they were married, the first would divorce the man	5	1.0
Don't know	29	5.6
If she doesn't know about it, it doesn't matter	126	24.4

8.10 And would the neighbors continue seeing the man in this case?

	N	%
No	131	22.7
Yes	379	65.7
Some yes, some no	1	.2
Sometimes yes, sometimes no	19	3.3
Other	3	.5
Don't know	44	7.6

	N	%

8.13. If the parents of a girl who is under age find out that she is having sexual relations with a man, what should they do?

	N	%
Nothing	22	3.6
Counsel her (reprimand included)	134	21.9
Throw her out	8	1.3
Send her to the countryside, to the family, etc.	4	.7
Try to make them marry	54	8.8
Resort to the authorities (includes such a resort to try to make them marry)	144	23.6
Other	29	4.7
Don't know	5	.8

8.14. And if the girl is having sexual relations with a boy who is also a minor, do you think that the parents of the girl would consider it a more serious matter, or less serious, or the same? (If more or less) Why?

	N	%
The same	102	16.7
More serious (unspecified)	68	11.1
More serious, since they can't be made to marry	96	15.7
More serious, since the boy would have trouble finding work	11	1.8
More serious (other reason)	256	42.0
Less serious (unspecified)	6	1.0
Less serious, since they are young and don't know what they are doing	41	6.7
Less serious (other reason)	19	3.1
Don't know	11	1.8

8.15. And in this case, of relations between minors, what do you think the parents of the girl would do?

	N	%
Nothing (includes "take them into the girl's house")	25	4.1
Counsel her (to stop)	88	14.5
Try to make them marry	160	26.4
Talk to the parents of the boy	57	9.4
Resort to the authorities (includes "intern the girl")	180	29.7
Keep her home until she is of age	35	5.8
Accept it if the boy is good, and if not, try to make them stop	6	1.0
Other	45	7.4
Don't know	11	1.8

		N	%

8.16. And in any of these cases in which a girl who is a minor has sexual relations, do you think that the birth of children should be avoided?

	N	%
No	407	68.9
Yes	159	26.9
Other	25	4.2

(If yes) How?

	N	%
Birth control method or device	70	53.8
Other	60	46.2

8.17. Suppose that a minor girl becomes pregnant. What do you think that her parents would do?

	N	%
Try to make them marry	209	34.4
Try to make the man responsible for the child	73	12.0
Ask help from the CVN	39	6.4
Accept the child, help the daughter (care for the child, etc.)	227	37.3
Throw her out	10	1.6
Hide her (send to countryside, etc.)	17	2.8
Other	27	4.4
Don't know	6	1.0

8.18. Do you believe that in such a case it would be better for the child not to be born?

	N	%
No (unspecified)	199	34.9
No, it is dangerous for the girl	16	2.8
No, let her live with the consequences	34	6.0
No, it is a crime, or sin	236	41.4
No, the child isn't to blame	37	6.5
No, the grandparents can care for the child	9	1.6
No, the child may amount to something in life	17	3.0
Yes (unspecified)	18	3.2
Yes, since the birth would damage the girl's status as single	4	.7

9.05. What does the junta do here? Projects of community development?

	N	%
No	24	5.8
Yes	343	83.1
Don't know	46	11.1

	N	%
Assign parcels (of land)?		
No	233	55.6
Yes	129	30.8
Don't know	57	13.6
Represent the barrio?		
No	29	6.9
Yes	322	77.0
Don't know	67	16.0
Aid in resolving disputes?		
No	123	29.7
Yes	216	52.2
Don't know	75	18.1
Has thrown out some bad neighbors		
No	291	70.6
Yes	46	11.2
Don't know	75	18.1
Has reserved land for a park or school		
No	116	28.4
Yes	247	60.4
Don't know	46	11.2
Has indicated where to throw trash, garbage		
No	109	26.1
Yes	281	67.4
Don't know	27	6.5
Has created a vigilance committee		
No	250	61.4
Yes	83	20.4
Don't know	74	18.2
What else does the junta do?		
Nothing else	229	61.4
Organizes parties	5	1.3
Has promoted a school	12	3.2
Organizes sports teams, ladies' committee	8	2.1
Aids with funerals	25	6.7
Other	61	16.4
Don't know	33	8.8

	N	%

9.06. Do you think the present junta is very active, a little active, inactive?

	N	%
Very active	193	46.6
A little active	148	35.7
Inactive	35	8.5
Don't know	34	8.2
Other	4	1.0

9.07. Do you consider that the activities of the junta here have been very good for the barrio, good, average, bad, or very bad? (reading categories)

	N	%
Very good	91	21.9
Good	168	40.5
Average (regular)	121	29.2
Bad	13	3.1
Very bad	6	1.4
Don't know	15	3.6
Other	1	.2

9.08. What do you think a resident of the barrio should do in order to improve it?

	N	%
Nothing (unspecified)	12	2.0
Nothing, only the government can improve it	15	2.6
Nothing, since I don't trust the junta (or the government)	11	1.9
Let everyone build (work) on his own; leave everyone else alone	84	14.3
Cooperate (generally)	265	45.2
Cooperate with the junta	101	17.2
Other	65	11.1
Don't know	33	5.6

9.09. Should the residents collaborate with the junta? (If yes) How?

	N	%
No	15	3.0
(If yes)		
Yes, if it's a good junta	12	2.4
Yes, with labor and money	334	66.5
Yes, following their directions	67	13.3
Yes, giving them ideas	9	1.8
Yes, cooperating with parties, raffles, etc., to get money for the barrio	7	1.4
Yes, if one can help	40	8.0
Yes, serving as a member of the junta	7	1.4
Don't know	11	2.2

117

		N	%

9.10. Have you or your spouse ever collaborated with the junta? (If yes) How?

	N	%
No (unspecified)	102	21.0
No, they haven't asked me	30	6.2
(If yes)		
With work or money	303	62.5
Following directions, attending meetings	14	2.9
Giving them ideas	2	.4
Cooperating with parties, raffles, etc.	11	2.3
Serving as member of the junta	14	2.9
Don't know	2	.4
If I have been able to help	7	1.4

9.11. Have you or your spouse ever held a position here in the barrio? (If yes) What?

	N	%
No	441	90.6
(If yes)		
President	9	1.8
Secretary or treasurer	16	3.3
Other office	16	3.3
Other answer	5	1.0

9.12. Would you or your spouse accept a position in the junta if you were elected or if it were offered?

	N	%
Yes	153	31.0
No (unspecified)	61	12.3
No, I don't have time	111	22.5
No, I can't (can't read, too old, sick, etc.)	59	11.9
No, it's too much responsibility (etc.)	21	4.3
No, I don't like such things	49	9.9
No, because people don't cooperate	4	.8
It depends; if others cooperate, yes	7	1.4
It depends (on how busy I am at work, or on the office offered)	29	5.9

10.03. More or less, how much do you spend monthly among all of you?

	N	%
Less than Bs. 300	96	17.1
Bs. 300-499	127	22.6
Bs. 500-799	164	29.1
Bs. 800-1, 199	112	19.9
Bs. 1,200-1,999	43	7.6
Bs. 2,000 or more	9	1.6
Not working now	12	2.1

	N	%

10.04 Type of house

	N	%
Block walls and concrete roof	148	25.1
Block walls and zinc (wood, asbestos) roof	203	34.4
Wood or adobe walls and zinc (etc.) roof	141	23.9
Carton walls and zinc (etc.) roof	98	16.6

Appendix C

Selected Questionnaire Items with Distribution of Responses by Age of Barrio

	I[1]		II		III	
	N	%	N	%	N	%
Age of head of the family:						
19-29	45	34.1	64	20.2	27	16.6
30-39	43	32.6	107	33.8	53	32.5
40-49	28	21.2	86	27.1	41	25.2
50-or older	16	12.1	60	18.9	42	25.7
Civil status of the head of the family (as stated by the interviewee):						
Bachelor (living in *concubinato*)	54	41.2	90	28.6	55	33.7
Bachelor (not living in *concubinato* in this house)	20	15.3	55	17.5	26	16.0
Married	48	36.6	130	41.3	65	39.9
Unido or *unida* (common-law marriage)	7	5.3	22	7.0	10	6.1
Widow(er)	2	1.5	17	5.4	6	3.7
Other (e.g., married to another man, but separated)	—	—	1	.3	1	.6
Occupation of the head of the family:						
Unskilled worker	42	33.6	69	22.1	46	29.9
Skilled worker	13	10.4	45	14.4	24	15.6
Comerciante (has own business)	6	4.8	13	4.2	5	3.2
Chauffeur, or unskilled white-collar employee (bill collector, shop salesman, messenger, office boy)	30	24.0	85	27.2	33	21.4

[1]The barrios were classified according to age into three types, ranging from I (youngest) to III (oldest). Barrios included in Type I are Cuatricentenario, Guzmán Blanco, and the upper portion of La Silsa; included, in Type II are Aguacaticos, El Desvío, the remainder of La Silsa, Niño Jesús, and Quebrada Catuche; included in Type III are La Amapola, Marín, and San Miguel.

	I		II		III	
	N	%	N	%	N	%
Skilled white-collar employee (secretary, cashier)	2	1.6	10	3.2	6	3.9
Street vendor	7	5.6	10	3.2	4	2.6
Professional (teacher, nurse)	3	2.4	5	1.6	3	1.9
Domestic	4	3.2	19	6.1	10	6.5
Sub-employment (ironing, making *arepas*, etc.)	—	—	5	1.6	3	1.9
Housewife	7	5.6	32	10.3	15	9.7
Public employment (e.g., policeman)	9	7.2	12	3.8	3	1.9
Other (includes student)	2	1.6	3	.9	1	.6
Don't know (or no answer)	—	—	4	1.3	1	.6

Whose house is this?

	N	%	N	%	N	%
Mine	107	81.1	197	62.9	79	48.5
Spouse of interviewee	13	9.8	30	9.6	7	4.3
Relative	9	6.8	28	8.9	22	13.5
Other person living in the barrio	1	.8	24	7.7	27	16.6
Other person living outside barrio	1	.8	30	9.6	26	16.0
Other	1	.8	4	1.3	2	1.2

Have you added any important additions to the house? ("Important" means ceiling, cement blocks, cement floor, another room.) If so, what?

	N	%	N	%	N	%
No	50	40.0	57	23.2	29	27.1
One important improvement	42	33.6	88	35.8	41	38.3
Two important improvements	20	16.0	48	19.5	23	21.5
Three or more important improvements	13	10.4	53	21.5	14	13.1

Where do you buy food?

	N	%	N	%	N	%
Within the barrio	26	19.5	96	30.6	92	56.8
Outside the barrio	97	72.9	191	60.8	64	39.5
Both within and outside the barrio	10	7.6	27	8.6	6	3.7

Do you always pay cash for food or does the storekeeper give you credit?

	N	%	N	%	N	%
Always buy for cash	102	77.9	232	73.2	111	68.1
Sometimes the *bodeguero* gives credit	20	15.3	65	20.5	35	21.5
Regularly the *bodeguero* gives credit	7	5.3	18	5.7	15	9.2
Other	2	1.5	2	.6	2	1.2

	I		II		III	
	N	%	N	%	N	%
If you have no money, would the storekeeper be inclined to give you credit?						
No	38	38.4	91	36.4	33	26.4
Yes	47	47.5	139	55.6	77	61.6
Don't know	12	12.1	18	7.2	13	10.4
Other	2	2.0	2	.8	2	1.0
More or less, how much do you spend monthly among all of you?						
Less than Bs. 300	25	20.3	44	15.3	27	17.8
Bs. 300-499	36	29.3	55	19.1	36	23.7
Bs. 500-799	41	33.3	83	28.8	40	26.3
Bs. 800-1,199	14	11.4	66	22.9	32	21.1
Bs. 1,200-1,999	3	2.4	29	10.1	11	7.2
Bs. 2,000 or more	—	—	6	2.1	3	2.0
Not working now	4	3.3	5	1.7	3	2.0
Type of house						
Block walls and concrete roof	6	4.7	91	21.9	51	32.5
Block walls and zinc (wood, asbestos) roof	22	17.1	116	38.2	65	41.4
Wood or adobe walls and zinc (etc.) roof	56	43.4	57	18.8	28	17.8
Carton walls and zinc (etc.) roof	45	34.9	40	13.2	13	8.3
Have you done anything so that your goods will pass to those persons to whom you would like to leave your belongings if you died?						
No	121	93.8	281	92.1	128	84.2
(If yes) The children are legitimate (recognized)	3	2.3	7	2.3	3	2.0
Life insurance, or bank account	3	2.3	2	.7	4	2.6
Will	2	1.6	5	1.6	7	4.6
I've talked with relatives (friends), and they will take care of the children	—	—	2	.7	—	—
Other	—	—	8	2.6	10	6.6

Index

Abortion, 39

Acción Democrática, 13, 49. *See also* Political
parties

Age: of barrios, 4, 11-16, 18-19, 42, 45, 67-70, 72,
120-122; of head of family related to age of
barrio, 67n; of interviewees and heads of
families, 91

Agency for International Development (AID), 29n

Aguaticos barrio, 15, 120n

Banks, borrowing from, 43-44, 106-107

Barriadas of Lima, 31

Barrio(s): studies of, 1; defined, 1n; backgrounds
of inhabitants of, 2, 10, 16, 75, 89-90;
development of, 4, 67-84; percentage of population in, 5; formation of, 6-8 (*see also*
Invasions); physical characteristics of, 8-9;
radio announcements regarding, 11; diversity
of, 12-16; eradication of, 29n, 74; related to
national life, 71; outlook of residents of,
75-83; classified according to type, 86-87;
motives for moving to, 90-91; age of (*see* Age,
of barrios)

Betancourt, Rómulo, 7, 29n

Bodegas, 42-43, 47, 68, 104, 121-122

Borrowing. *See* Credit system; Loans

Caciquismo, 49n

Caracas: description and population of, 5, 8;
barrios of, 5-7, 12-16, 84 and *passim*

Change: in the barrio, 67-70; and law, 72-84

Children: number of, per household, 11; illegitimate, 32, 39, 40, 69n, 79, 115; support of, in
termination of marriage, 37-38; percentage of,
in the population, 38; parents' obligations
toward, 39-41, 79, and inheritance, 41, 71,
103, education levels attained by, 93; recognition of, 93. *See also* Juvenile gangs;
Venezuelan Children's Council

Civil status of barrio residents, 92

Colinas de las Acacias, 52

Commercial enterprises, 9. See also *Bodegas*; Credit
system; Loans

Committee to Remodel the Barrios (CRB), 29n

Common Law, 53. *See also* Law

Communications, mass, 11

Contraception, 39, 115

Cooperation. *See* Junta, and cooperative or public
works

Cost of living, 12, 118, 122

Courts, barrio reliance on, 47, 105, 106

Credit system, 42-44, 68, 72, 77, 104, 121-122

Crime, 46-47, 52, 54. *See also* Disturbance of the
peace; Fighting; Juvenile gangs; Police;
Security of person and property; Theft

Cuatricentenario barrio, 16, 120n

CVN. *See* Venezuelan Children's Council

Development, related to the legal system, 73-84

Disputes, settlement of, 53-54, 72, 109, 116

Education, 9, 11, 15, 39-40, 71, 72n, 82, 108;
husband's obligations regarding, 35; and age of
barrio, 68, 70; level of, attained by heads of
family, 92-93; junta role in, 116

El Desvío barrio, 14, 120n

Electricity, 9, 15

Emergency Plan of 1958, 7, 29, 74, 81

Employment, 68, 70, 94. *See also* Occupations;
Unemployment

Explusion, as a sanction, 22, 54, 116

Extended family, 31, 78-79, *See also* Family;
Nuclear family

Family, 10-11, 31-41, 54, 69, 78-79; incomes of, in La Chivera, 16

Fatalism versus rationality, 75-76

Favelas of Rio de Janeiro, 7, 8

Fighting, 71, 107-108. *See also* Juvenile gangs

Food shopping, 104, 121. See also *Bodegas*

Gangs. *See* Juvenile gangs

Gómez, Juan Vicente, 17

Government: policy of, toward barrios, 6-7, 9, 28-29, 48; land owned by, 17; barrio attitude toward, 78, 84, 97, 99, 108-109. *See also* Emergency Plan of 1958; Law, national; *Superbloques*

Guzmán Blanco barrio, 15-16

Hagen, Everett, 81

Head of family, 2, 6, 10, 31, 67n, 72, 91-93, 120

Hornos de Cal barrio, 16

Houses, 5, 8-10, 13-16, 71; number of occupants in, 9, 91, 95-96; ownership of, 17-18, 20, 25, 26, 32, 67, 69, 71-72, 76, 97-99, 102-103, 121; construction of, 20, 78, 101; sale of, 22-23; inheritance of, 23; improvement of, 27, 29-30, 72-75, 81, 101, 102, 121; allocation of, in termination of marriage, 38; and the junta, 52; types of, 119, 122. *See also* Ranchos; *Superbloques*

Husbands (legal or common law), obligations of, 32-34, 36, 110

Illegitimacy. *See* Children, illegitmate

Income: related to age of barrio, 68; and deferment of gratification, 82; of households, 97; *See also* Cost of living

Independence, 80

Infidelity, 33-34, 36, 69n, 112-113

Inheritance, 23, 41, 71, 79, 103-104, 122

Invasions, 6, 18-19, 21, 48

Jefatura (municipal council), 99, 105, 109

Junta: sanctioning power of, 4, 54; national, 7; and cooperative or public works, 9, 12, 48-52, 69, 72, 76-78, 83; of San Miguel barrio, 13; of Niño Jesús barrio, 14-15; of La Silsa barrio, 15; of Cuatricentenario barrio, 16; and land rights, 19-20, 28, 52-53, 72; dispute-resolving functions of, 21-22, 53-54; and trash disposal, 22-23, 53, 116; and rentals, 24-25, 52-53; and security of the person, 46; election to and term of office in, 49; barrio attitude toward, 51-52; role of, related to age of barrio, 69, 84; and individual independence, 80; questionnaire responses regarding, 97, 99, 105, 106, 108, 109, 115-118

Juvenile gangs, 13, 46, 69. *See also* Crime; Fighting

La Amapola barrio, 12, 120n

La Bandera barrio, 14

La Charneca barrio, 16, 52

La Chivera. *See* Guzmán Blanco barrio

Land tenure, 5-7, 17-20, 25-30, 52, 67, 72-75, 81; questionnaire responses regarding, 97, 98-99, 102, 116

La Silsa barrio, 15, 120n

La Vega parish, 12

Law: nature of, in the barrios, 1-3, 72; national, 23, 24, 26, 32, 40, 43, 71, 80n; common, 53; relationship of, to development in the barrio, 73-84

Leoni, President, 29n

Lima, *barriadas* of, 31

Limited good, concept of, 76-77

Literacy, 11. *See also* Education

Loans, 43-44, 106-107

Marín barrio, 13, 120n

Marriage: obligations in, 32-37, 110-111; termination of, 37; and the status of women, 80

Mercado libre, 104

Migration and barrio settlement, 6-7. *See also* Urbanization

Mobility, barrio attitudes regarding, 94

Municipal council. See *Jefatura*

SAM/PSE EH/124 SCLSS
LKARST